Mordecai Richler: A Life in Ten Novels

Mordecai Richler: A Life in Ten Novels

Ada Craniford

iUniverse, Inc.
New York Lincoln Shanghai

Mordecai Richler: A Life in Ten Novels

Copyright © 2005 by Ada Craniford

All rights reserved. No part of this book may be used or reproduced by any means, graphic, electronic, or mechanical, including photocopying, recording, taping or by any information storage retrieval system without the written permission of the publisher except in the case of brief quotations embodied in critical articles and reviews.

iUniverse books may be ordered through booksellers or by contacting:

iUniverse
2021 Pine Lake Road, Suite 100
Lincoln, NE 68512
www.iuniverse.com
1-800-Authors (1-800-288-4677)

ISBN-13: 978-0-595-37208-9 (pbk)
ISBN-13: 978-0-595-81607-1 (ebk)
ISBN-10: 0-595-37208-2 (pbk)
ISBN-10: 0-595-81607-X (ebk)

Printed in the United States of America

For Doug and Karen and Eric

Contents

Acknowledgements ix
Preface xi
Introduction: Thrust and Parody 1
Chronology: Richler's Life and Novels 9
The Acrobats: A Mocking Salute 19
Son of a Smaller Hero: Before the Deluge 28
A Choice of Enemies: A Bad Choice 39
The Apprenticeship of Duddy Kravitz: A Parody of Success 50
The Incomparable Atuk: Making the Punishment Fit the Crime . . 63
Cocksure: An Honest Man in a Nightmare World 77
St. Urbain's Horseman: Shoveling Trouble in the Stables of the Lord 87
Joshua Then and Now: Bridging the Gap 98
Solomon Gursky Was Here: Biography as Quest 110
Barney's Version: Summing Up 122
Afterword 139
Bibliography 141
Index 159

Acknowledgements

A deep debt of gratitude to my editor and friend, Jean Paton, who saw me through every stage of writing this book. Her encouragement, advice, and critical eye kept me from faltering time and time again.

Very special thanks to Michael Levine for giving generously of his time, for getting publishing permission from Florence Richler, and for having the manuscript academically critiqued.

I am grateful to my son, Eric Weinthal, who helped me find my focus and gave valuable suggestions for improving individual chapters.

Many thanks to William Weintraub for allowing me to read his collection of Richler's letters, and for answering questions about events in Richler's life.

Malcolm Lester read an early version of the manuscript, as did Ruth and Eric Miller.

Marlys Chevrefils, at the MacKimmie Library, University of Calgary, responded speedily to e-mails asking for additional information from the Richler Collection.

Finally, extra special thanks to my husband, Doug, who put up with the anxieties that went with writing this book, rescued me each time the computer tried to do me in, and took charge of the line-editing and proofreading.

Certain central ideas in *Mordecai Richler: A Life in Ten Novels* will also be found in my previous book on Mordecai Richler.

Preface

Thoughtful, funny, always controversial, Richler has entertained, amused, and outraged us in his short stories, children's books, collections of essays, and articles for newspapers and magazines. But serious readers know that the ten novels most clearly reveal the essence of his art; and Richler has frequently stated that it is by these novels that he hopes to be remembered.

After fourteen years of teaching Richler's novels, both to high school and university students, at a time when his reputation was nowhere near as great as it is now, I wrote a book called *Fiction and Fact in Mordecai Richler's Novels* (published by The Edwin Mellen Press in 1992). The main purpose of that book was to show that those who were writing about Richler's novels—literary critics, journalists, and reviewers—were ignoring some of the fascinating things that were going on beneath every surface story line. Because Richler was not forthcoming about his writing methods, and because his stories were both realistic and satiric, critics and reviewers for the most part ignored his playful reworking of classical myth, biblical narrative, and certain famous novels, plays, and poems. When on occasion some literary borrowing was noticed—for example in articles about *The Acrobats*—it was dismissed as "pastiche" (a superficial form of imitation). In later books it was seen as a lazy man's "recycling" of material, both his own and that of other writers. At no time was it suspected that Richler had a special reason for his so-called recycling: that he was doing it for the purpose of parody, to acknowledge and re-evaluate a previous work, directing the reader back to the original to perhaps think it through again.

> At heart I'm an arranger still, whose chiefest literary pleasure is to take a received melody—an old narrative poem, a classical myth, a shopworn literary convention, a shard of my experience…and,

> *improvising like a jazzman within its constraints, re-orchestrate it to present purpose.* (John Barth, quoted by Linda Hutcheon in *A Theory of Parody* 1985. 36)

If Richler had told us that he, like John Barth, was by inclination and talent "an arranger," "improvising like a jazzman" on his own life and on the writings of those he admired, I would never have had to write either my first book or the present one. But, although he was frank about many things Richler was cagey about the way he wrote; and in consequence readers are still missing out on some of the most exciting aspects of his writing.

Perhaps because I grew up in Montreal at the same time as Mordecai Richler (even dating boys who went to his old high school Baron Byng, although not Richler himself); and perhaps because I seem to have read many of the same books that he did, I began noticing that he was re-working in unusual ways certain parts of novels and poems from our common reading experience. His use of biblical names and of certain stories from the Bible (far more than critics and reviewers had noticed), struck me as especially odd and worthy of further exploration.

In the years after my first book was published, Richler wrote his tenth novel, *Barney's Version*. This and Richler's untimely death made me want to revisit all ten of the novels to see how they would read as a completed life's work. What impressed me most profoundly was that Richler, from first to last, was writing parody—as defined by Samuel Johnson and noted by Linda Hutcheon in *A Theory of Parody*—as "a kind of writing, in which the words of an author or his thoughts are taken, and by a slight change adapted to some new purpose."(Hutcheon, 36)

Armed with Linda Hutcheon's magnificent analysis of the various forms of parody, I plunged more deeply into Richler's ten novels. This time I observed not only the literary and autobiographical currents that flowed through each book, but also the many ways he would diverge from a well-known source. These divergences, blended into his own work of fiction, cast new light on works taken from our common literary heritage while revealing in intimate detail the ways that Richler himself viewed the world.

Introduction: Thrust and Parody

In *The Acrobats,* his first published novel, Richler immediately establishes himself as a witty writer of parody. And he is immediately misunderstood. What many critics considered a lack of originality and simple imitation of (among others) Hemingway, Celine, T.S. Eliot, W.H. Auden, and Henry Miller, is Richler's way of paying homage to his literary predecessors while at the same time placing himself in their midst. But parody is more than simple imitation: it includes both homage and critical distance, "activation of the past by giving it a new and often ironic context" (Hutcheon, 5). So in *The Acrobats,* Richler imitates Hemingway in his settings and characters, while caricaturing his romantic obsessions at the same time. For example in Hemingway's famous novel *The Sun also Rises,* the hero Jake Barnes has suffered a war wound that prevents him from making love. In *The Acrobats,* Richler reprises and mocks this predicament through one of the minor characters, the pathetic Derek Lawson. Unlike Hemingway's hero who refers only obliquely to the physical location of his wound, Derek gets right up front and personal:

> *'Yes, I was in the war.' And he stood up, pale and shivering and giggling, clutching the crotch of his pants in his fist. 'I was wounded three times. The last time—Here!' then uncorked misery wringing his face, his raving soul unzipped, naked, he collapsed in his chair.* (*Acrobats,* 124)

Through this grotesque parody of Jake Barnes's quiet suffering, Richler mocks Hemingway's idealization of battle and the wounds acquired in war. But even while he distances himself from Hemingway's worship of wounded heroes, he acknowledges his debt to Hemingway with a wistfully mangled reference to another one of the master's famous novels:

> 'As a matter of fact,' Andre said, 'I'm not a painter at all. I came here to study life in its entirety. One day I hope to write a book about it. You know, like that Who do the bells toll for…Meanwhile I make ends meet peddling hashish at convent doors.' (12)

Here Richler mocks mainly himself—since at the time of writing *The Acrobats* he was a penniless would-be novelist in Europe, daring to hope that one day he would be as good a writer as Hemingway—with a book as well known as *For Whom the Bell Tolls*.

While Hemingway's style and characters are at once celebrated and mocked in the early chapters of *The Acrobats*, the last section of Richler's novel parodies another writer's famous book: Malcolm Lowry's *Under the Volcano* (1947). We are alerted to this borrowing by the sudden sound of a disembodied voice that proclaims: "The corpse will have to be shipped back to America for Mama." This imitates the unexpected intrusion of a voice booming out of a loudspeaker in *Under the Volcano*: "A corpse will be transported by express." In both novels, the voice suddenly breaks in to foreshadow the oncoming death of the drunken, guilt-ridden protagonist. But Richler's version refers to yet another layer of parody in *The Acrobats*, because the central character Andre is given unmistakable Christ-like attributes. This places our mental image of Andre's corpse being shipped back to Mama in the context of the many artistic renderings of the Virgin Mary's desolation at the death of her son Jesus—including Michelangelo's marble *Pieta* where the dead Jesus is lying in her lap. Since Andre's mother in *The Acrobats* is notably promiscuous, the echoing is decidedly ironic. That Malcolm Lowry also intimated that his drunken death-seeking hero had Christ-like attributes, increases Richler's debt to the earlier book.

After *The Acrobats* with its multi-storied parody (of which I've only mentioned two), Richler settles down to a series of novels in which he parodies Bible stories. In these novels he signals the borrowings by the names of his characters and by the ways they follow in their namesakes' footsteps—invariably with a critical difference. In *Son of a Smaller Hero*, he names the protagonist "Noah" and sends him sailing off to Europe at the end of the book, leaving his mother to die of a heart attack metaphorically depicted as drowning.

> *Sweat streamed down her face. Her skin turned grey. A gathering fog of exploding yellow lights, and Leah reached up wearily but in vain for a fading retreating Noah before she was washed back down under many, heavy seas.... Her head throbbed. A vice-like pain twisted, tightened, in her chest. Tighter and tighter.* (204)

Richler's Noah saves himself by sailing off alone, leaving friends and family behind. The biblical Noah sailed away, taking only his wife and sons (and of course the paired animals) into the ark, leaving the rest of the human world to drown. By working key elements of the Bible story into a fictionalized version of his own growing up and shipping out, Richler passes judgment on the biblical Noah, on his own fictional Noah, and on himself. The Bible story showed God saving a righteous man and his immediate family, and destroying everyone else. At no time did it suggest that Noah had compassion for the people who were left to drown, nor did he make any attempt to save them. Richler's Noah worries about his mother and about abandoning his mistress whom he no longer loves. He wretchedly wonders, "What do you do with used people? Send them to the cleaners?" Richler creates ironic distance between his story and its biblical source. Both Noahs sail away, but Richler shows us in detail what happens to the people left on shore, and the conflicted emotions of the one who leaves them behind.

Survival and guilt are major themes in Richler's novels. The cost of saving oneself alone involves remorse at the thought of those who are not saved. And this taints the excitement of moving on. Richler is constantly aware of the conundrum posed by Rabbi Hillel in his treatise on the Talmud:

> *If I am not for myself, who is for me?*
> *And if I am for myself alone, what am I?*
> *And if not now, when?*

Personal survival and becoming a success, at great cost to oneself and great hurt to people one loves, is the theme of Richler's much praised fourth novel: *The Apprenticeship of Duddy Kravitz*. It tells the story of a boy "born with a rusty spoon in his mouth" who acquires a prime piece of land by hard work, perseverance, and cheating a trusted friend. The acme of his achievement is running a crippled but powerful local drug lord off his land, thereby finally gaining the respect of his own taxi-driving pimp of a father. *The Apprenticeship of Duddy Kravitz* gains its strength from two literary sources that Richler parodies and blends: the Bible story of David and Goliath, and Budd Schulberg's brilliantly successful novel *What makes Sammy Run?*. "Duddy" is a Jewish nickname for "David," and the David-side of Duddy Kravitz makes him strong and resourceful, loving and loyal to his family, and in his own small way a "giant-killer." But his crass nature (revealed by his actions and the sound of his surname); his being hailed as "Sammy Glick" by one of his classmates; and the many echoes of Budd Schulberg's novel that we hear in Duddy's story, all point to Schulberg's *What Makes Sammy Run?*. And it is the fusion of Richler's two sources that makes us (as one critic put it) applaud Duddy's achievements with only one hand, while we enthusiastically applaud Richler's achievement with two. The parody of David and Goliath is so impeccably fused with the parody of *What Makes Sammy Run?* that Richler's novel was considered to be completely true to life, and became his first literary success.

After making a name for himself with *Duddy Kravitz*, Richler proceeds to savage his celebrity with the first of his bleak, black satires: *The Incomparable Atuk*. Satire is the form that parody takes when it viciously ridicules a part of society in the hope of bringing about social change. And in

Atuk, Richler takes on the Toronto cultural elite and the whole concept of literary celebrity, mocking himself at the same time. As Gustave Flaubert is known to have said, "Madame Bovary c'est moi," so—on one level of *The Incomparable Atuk*—the main character represents Richler in the first flush of his celebrity, which still leaves him scrambling for money. The novel is an "Eskimo" parody and fusion of Budd Schulberg's *What Makes Sammy Run?* and Richler's *The Apprenticeship of Duddy Kravitz,* with sidelong glances at its newly famous, still poverty stricken author. Atuk loses his head at the end of the book after being tricked into taking part in a crooked get-rich-quick television quiz show. The show is called "Stick out your neck" which Atuk foolishly does. This double-edged warning that Richler aims at rigged quiz shows, phony celebrities, and the pseudo-artistic community that supports them, includes advice to himself not to take anything his critics say too seriously. He has already found out that he will be praised and blamed for the wrong things and his anger at being misunderstood partly fuels the savagery of his satire.

Everything about *The Incomparable Atuk* is heavily ironic, including the title that suggests Atuk is unique. On the contrary, he is in fact a Duddy Kravitz stripped of his David side; a more venal and criminal Sammy Glick; a Mordecai Richler without his talent, scruples, or love for family and friends. There is, however, one way that Atuk does stand alone: he never at any time or under any condition feels a single pang of guilt. His singular lack of remorse covers the killing and eating of an American colonel and the persuading of his naïve brother Mush Mush that the red light at a busy traffic intersection means *Go*. In this respect he is unlike any of Richler's other protagonists who suffer profoundly, even for things they are only minimally responsible for.

In fact every one of Richler's protagonists (except for *The Incomparable Atuk*) carries a burden of guilt that is punished according to the literary and personal sources Richler weaves into the novel. In *A Choice of Enemies* his central character leads a life of unfulfilled emotional prudence borrowed from T.S. Eliot's "The Love song of J. Alfred Prufrock." He is also more or less an anti-Semite as was Eliot himself. At the end of the story he makes a hasty, ill-advised marriage, as both Richler and Eliot did, and he is already casting his eye on the woman living upstairs.

Gentile protagonists in Richler's novels either die or end up badly diminished, while his Jewish main characters come out more or less intact—except for Barney Panofsky in Richler's final novel, *Barney's Version*. Survival is guaranteed for the Jewish characters by their biblical names and the Bible story that underlies the plot: a source of protection that Barney—created in Richler's ailing old age—unfortunately lacks. Although *Barney's Version* includes a playful parody of Saul Bellow's *Herzog*—in which the main character tries to make sense of the events leading up to his present miserable state—*Barney's Version* also brings back some of Richler's previous fictional characters interwoven with events from his own past. To keep us from taking Barney's decline more seriously than he intends, Richler inserts a ridiculous murder charge that is finally resolved only with the help of a mysterious airplane that flies straight out of Bellow's novel.

As Richler's first satire, *The Incomparable Atuk* savages the Toronto cultural and pseudo-cultural scene, so his second satire *Cocksure* takes on the publishing and film industries of London, England. The term "cocksure" indicates a state of swaggering self-confidence that Richler's protagonist sadly lacks. It is, however, abundantly present in those who bring about the hero's doom.

After two wildly extravagant, viciously funny satires, Richler returns to the fictionalized autobiographical style of *Son of a Smaller Hero*. The protagonist of *St. Urbain's Horseman* again has a biblical name but he is not the horseman of the title. He is named "Jacob" after the biblical Jacob (son of Isaac) who stole his brother Esau's blessing. While Richler was writing *St. Urbain's Horseman*, his own father (Moses Isaac Richler) was dying of cancer; and in the novel the fictional Jacob tricks his dying father Issy (Isaac) into blessing him. This parody, rather than denigrating the biblical source, lends dignity to Jacob Hersh's otherwise profoundly foolish behavior.

Joshua Then and Now, following *St. Urbain's Horseman* by nine years, parodies the famous battles of Joshua who led the Israelites into the Promised Land, putting to the sword every man, woman, and child who stood in their way. In this book the parody, while acknowledging the need for battle, implicitly criticizes the Bible's excessive killing; and Richler's Joshua suffers for his immoderate acts of revenge. *Joshua Then and Now* is filled with battles that leave Joshua, its dauntless hero, a slowly recovering casualty of war.

Richler's second to last book *Solomon Gursky Was Here,* aside from spoofing the World War II graffiti message "Kilroy Was Here," peppers the scene with parodies. The main one concerns the history of the Gurskys, based squarely on Peter C. Newman's *Bronfman Dynasty* along with whatever Richler knew about the Montreal founders of the Seagram Empire. Keeping large swaths of critical distance between his version of the story and Newman's, Richler creates a special Bronfman brother whom he calls Solomon. This brother is symbolically linked to yet another book, *The Quest for Corvo* by A.J.A. Symons (which Richler specifically mentions in his novel). By combining his two main sources and others that he acknowledges as research material, Richler creates a multi-layered tall tale about the rise of a powerful family, and its self-fueled decline.

Finally, *Barney's Version,* the last novel Richler wrote, parodies characters and events from a number of his previous novels as well as situations and people taken from his life. At the same time it expropriates significant chunks from Saul Bellow's novel *Herzog,* a book that focuses on Herzog's attempts to deal with the betrayals of his latest wife. The *Herzog* connection broadens the terms in which we view Barney's lament for his mismanaged life, making it part of a larger literary tradition.

Although Richler insisted at every opportunity that his novels were not to be read as autobiography, he also, in an early essay, pointed ruefully at his biofictional technique.

> ...*too often, I think, it is we who are the fumbling, the misfits, <u>but unmistakably lovable</u> heroes of our very own fiction, triumphant in our vengeful imaginations as we never were in actuality.* ("A Sense of the Ridiculous," in *Notes on an Endangered Species and Others*) (1974).

That Richler wrote about himself and his family, transparently disguised, is well known although the extent and cleverness of his fictionalizing has not been appreciated. But the biographical threads, fascinating as they are, still make up only a part of the complicated web of literary sources and pure invention out of which Richler created his ten novels. By teasing out the various strands that go into each novel, we follow the process of literary creation and the evolving of his life. Since parody (imitation with a difference) is Richler's usual method, we look closely at each strand of parody. What is he saying about the books he has read, the life he has lived, the beliefs he holds or discards? We especially notice the way he parodies himself along with his fictional heroes. We follow the changes in his life story, in his fictional characters, and in the outside sources of which he avails himself, as we move from book to book—until we see it all mockingly summarized in *Barney's Version* at the end of his novel-writing life.

Chronology: Richler's Life and Novels

1931
Mordecai Richler was born on January 27, 1931, the second son of an ultra-orthodox Jewish family living on St. Urbain Street in Montreal. The arranged marriage of his parents, Moses Isaac Richler and Leah Rosenberg, had been unhappy from the start—at least partly because of the difference in their social status. Leah, the daughter of a renowned rabbi looked down on her husband, a driver in his family's scrap yard.

1944
When Richler was thirteen everything in his life changed. Soon after he celebrated his Bar Mitzvah and "became a man" in the eyes of the Jewish community, his mother left his father, having fallen in love (according to her autobiography) with a man she met at night school. Richler entered Baron Byng High School, gave up practicing Judaism and started playing snooker instead. In the summer he and his older brother, Avrum, helped their mother run a boarding house she bought in the Laurentians. At the same time he became estranged from his father. "Shortly after the marriage annulment, I fought with my father. Fists flew. We didn't speak for two years." He did badly at high school, but was accepted at Sir George Williams (now Concordia) University.

1948
While still attending Sir George Williams, Richler worked as a part-time reporter for the *Montreal Herald*. His brother Avrum went to The University of Montreal and eventually became an optometrist in St. John's, Newfoundland.

1951

At nineteen Richler left university without getting his degree. He boarded a ship from Montreal and began his travels to Europe. He said that "things in Gay Paree were uncommonly lousy. [He] had contracted scurvy, of all things, from not eating sufficient fruit or vegetables." He also said that in Paris he inhabited a rat-infested room at the Grand Hotel Excelsior, and declared it had served as a brothel for the Nazi Wehrmacht during the war. While in Paris he sold his first short story "Shades of Darkness" to *Points* magazine for ten dollars. Later he went to Spain, and on the Spanish island of Ibiza he wrote the first draft of what would become his first published novel, *The Acrobats*—now thought to be based on an earlier unpublished manuscript, *The Rotten People*.

1952

Having received money from his father for a ticket home, Richler left *The Acrobats* with publisher Andre Deutsch in London and then returned to Montreal. Here his journalist friend William Weintraub helped him get a job writing morning radio newscasts for the Canadian Broadcasting Corporation.

1953

After less than a year in Canada, Richler returned to London with his girlfriend, Cathy Boudreau. They were married a year later in spite of his own misgivings and against the advice of close friends. The marriage ended in 1958.

1954

The Acrobats was published in London by Andre Deutsch and in New York by G.P. Putnam's Sons. It was widely reviewed for a first novel, but damned by many critics who misunderstand the author's intentions.

Set in Spain and dedicated to Richler's mother, The Acrobats is a novel with a deeply troubled hero. Andre Bennet is a morose, idealistic, confused young man who lives in a rat-infested hotel room; drinks himself into hallucinations; and suffers from migraines. An American woman, old enough to be his mother, tries to seduce him. But Andre is in love with the young dancer Toni who may or may not be a prostitute, but who is definitely sleeping with a former Nazi, Reinhold Kraus. Andre doesn't know about Kraus's relationship with Toni. But since he is still staggering under a heavy load of guilt because of a former girlfriend's abortion and death, he is ambivalent about marrying her. At the end of the story, when Andre is ready to be happy at last, he and Kraus have a deadly confrontation.

1955

Richler's second novel, *Son of a Smaller Hero*, was published by Andre Deutsch to generally favorable reviews. However, the Montreal Jewish community reacted with outrage to what it perceived as an unflattering portrait of Montreal Jews.

Set in Montreal, and covering the time between summer 1952 and winter 1954, <u>Son of a Smaller Hero</u> was originally dedicated to Richler's first wife, Cathy—a dedication that was left out of later editions. The story begins with the twenty-year-old protagonist Noah Adler living away from home for the first time. He has turned away from the rituals of Orthodox Judaism thereby antagonizing his entire family, especially the rigidly religious grandfather Melech who owns the family scrap yard and keeps a tight control over his children and grandchildren. Away from his family, lonely and insecure, Noah is befriended by Theo a professor at his university, whose kindness he repays by running off with Miriam, the professor's wife. Noah's passion soon subsides, but still he offers to marry Miriam who, to his great relief, refuses. When Noah's father dies in a fire, his mother, who has long despised her husband, tries to make Noah come back home to take care of her. But Noah breaks away, and by the end of the novel, at the age of twenty-two, he boards a ship and sails for Europe.

1957

At some point between 1955 and 1957, Richler and his wife Cathy shared a villa in Roquebrun near Monte Carlo with good friends—film-writer/producer Stanley Mann and his beautiful wife Florence, a fashion model. At the villa, both marriages unraveled. Cathy went away; Stanley Mann went back to England; and Richler and Florence came together in what would become a lifelong union. Until he was able to marry Florence, Richler shared lodgings on the top floor of a crumbling, condemned Victorian building in London with fellow expatriate Ted Kotcheff, a promising television director with whom he later made three successful films. At this time Richler, who was chronically in debt, agreed to rewrite a film script called *Room at the Top* for which he was well paid but received no screen credit. Later, he and Kotcheff would work together on the sequel, *Life at the Top*.

1957

Richler's third novel *A Choice of Enemies* was published by Andre Deutsch in London, and McClelland and Stewart in Canada. The reviews were quite good but not overly enthusiastic.

Set in London in the 1950s and dedicated to Joyce Weiner (Richler's literary agent), A Choice of Enemies centers on Norman Price, a 38 year old Canadian film writer living in London who befriends Ernst Haupt, a young, illegal refugee from East Germany. Norman's friends all turn against him because of Ernst, and Ernst steals Norman's girlfriend Sally. After losing his friends, his girl, and finally his job, Norman develops amnesia. He ends up marrying a homely, malicious woman who looked after him when he didn't know who he was. Without Norman's protection, Ernst is forced to leave London. He goes to Canada where he is blackmailed into marrying an unpleasant woman from whom he had bought identity papers. Sally, abandoned by her two lovers, stages a melodramatic suicide that accidentally succeeds.

1959

The Apprenticeship of Duddy Kravitz was published by Andre Deutsch in London; Little, Brown and Company in Boston; and McClelland and Stewart in Toronto. Rave reviews impressed the Montreal Jewish Community though there was still concern about the way Jews were portrayed. Richler was awarded a Canada Council Junior Arts Fellowship.

Set in Montreal and dedicated to Florence whose divorce came through in 1959, The Apprenticeship of Duddy Kravitz tells the story of a nobody who becomes a somebody by acquiring a large piece of land in the Laurentians. Throwing moral scruples aside in his rush to success, Duddy Kravitz loses the love of his girlfriend Yvette and the approval of his beloved grandfather to whom he had always turned for affection and advice. At the end of the story, Duddy has acquired his land and won his father's long-sought approval, but the other losses diminish his triumph.

1960

Richler married Florence and adopted Florence and Stanley's son Daniel. Ted Kotcheff (Richler's former housemate) was best man at the wedding. Mordecai and Florence soon began producing the rest of their family: Noah, Emma, Martha and Jacob. Except for brief periods away, the Richlers lived in London until 1972.

1963

The Incomparable Atuk was published by McClelland and Stewart to the consternation of Toronto's cultural elite who found themselves scandalously satirized. Montrealers hailed the novel as a great work of art.

Set in Toronto and dedicated to Richler's father, The Incomparable Atuk is a bold, black satire. It offers thinly veiled caricatures of prominent Torontonians, who are hoodwinked by a greasy, smelly "Eskimo" poet who unaccountably has their women-folk in thrall. Atuk, who lives and dies on the cutting edge of the entertainment world, becomes wildly popular as artist and lover to the cultural crowd. He is called an "Eskimo" but his father, brothers and sisters whom he has brought to Toronto with him (and locked in a basement apartment where they churn out ugly, misshapen pieces of "Eskimo art") consider themselves to be the "Chosen Pagans." Meanwhile the father of a Jewish family turns out to be a crazed anti-Gentile who exchanges babies' identity bracelets at the Christian Temperance Hospital in an effort to prove that all Gentiles look alike.

1967

Richler's father died of cancer. Richler sent support money to Sara, his father's second wife and now his widow. A rift developed between Richler and his brother Avrum.

1968

Cocksure was published by Simon and Schuster in the United States and Canada. This very funny, "down and dirty" satire on British publishing and film conglomerates was dashed off—according to Richler—while he was working on *St. Urbain's Horseman*. To everyone's surprise, *Cocksure* won the Governor General's Award, Canada's top literary prize.
That same year Richler and his family spent a year in Canada. He had been appointed writer-in-residence at Sir George Williams University in Montreal—the university from which he had never graduated.

Cocksure mocks the London film and publishing worlds by pitting a kind and gentle Gentile named Mortimer Griffin against three grotesque antagonists: Shalinsky a maniacal Jew; Ziggy a physically disgusting homewrecker; and Star Maker a man who makes "virtual" movie stars. The tearing down of a decent man is not funny; but the insanely satiric dirty jokes that abound in the book make us laugh.

1971

Richler's long awaited "big book" *St. Urbain's Horseman* was published by McClelland and Stewart to wide acclaim, winning him his second Governor General's Award.

Richler's first wife Cathy Boudreau developed cancer while living as a nun in a Buddhist community in Taiwan. After her recovery she moved to Toronto where, according to Richler, she worked at a summer camp and as a waitress.

Acknowledging Florence as his "first reader," Richler dedicates St. Urbain's Horseman *"To Florence and my other editors." In the novel, Jacob Hersh is a successful film director living in London with his adored wife and children. Feeling unworthy of his own good fortune, he decides to befriend his accountant—a repulsive little man called Harry Stein to whom he unaccountably lends his house. As a result of this generous gesture, he and Harry are brought up on sex charges in London's Old Bailey court. Meanwhile the Horseman of the story—a fantasy figure projected on Jacob's cousin Joey—is imagined to be valiantly defending Jews and hunting Nazis all over the world.*

1972
With their four younger children—Noah, Emma, Martha and Jacob—Richler and Florence made the big move back to Canada, leaving Daniel behind to finish his exams. They acquired a house in the Westmount district of Montreal and a cottage in the Eastern Townships. Richler joined the editorial board of the American Book-of-the-Month Club and took on the position of Visiting Professor at Carlton University in Ottawa.

1974
Richler collaborated on the movie version of *The Apprenticeship of Duddy Kravitz* with friend and former housemate, Ted Kotcheff, Richler writing the screenplay and Kotcheff directing. The film won the Screenwriters Guild of America Award and was nominated for an Academy Award: a big step forward for the Canadian film industry.

1980
Joshua Then and Now, Richler's "homecoming" book, was published by McClelland and Stewart and dedicated to Ted Kotcheff.

The setting of <u>Joshua Then and Now</u> is Montreal and the Eastern Townships. Joshua Shapiro, physically and emotionally shattered in the "Now" of the book, is on his way to recovery at the end. During his painfully slow recuperation, he tries to figure out how he got into such a mess, and what he can do about it. As Joshua looks at his life before and after his return to Montreal, he revisits old battles and fights some new ones. His father Reuben—a prizefighter as a young man who later worked as debt collector for the mob—displays an astonishing, hilarious familiarity with the King James Bible. Joshua's mother Esther becomes a strip tease artist and porno star.

1981

Richler's mother wrote a memoir called *The Errand Runner: Reflections of a Rabbi's Daughter*, published by John Wiley and Sons. The book mainly eulogized her parents, especially her father, Rabbi Rosenberg, whom she revered and adored. Only toward the end of the book did she set forth in sordid detail the story of her unfortunate arranged marriage to Moses Isaac Richler; her bitterness toward the whole Richler family; and some of her amorous relationships. Mordecai Richler was furious at this public airing of private family affairs. He dissociated himself from his mother and remained estranged until her death. He did not attend her funeral.

1989

Richler's second to last novel *Solomon Gursky Was Here* was published by the Penguin Group in Canada, England, the United States, Australia and New Zealand. Immediately linked to the Canadian Bronfman family of Seagram's fame, it was called "a stunning triumph of the imagination." After hearing about something called "inter-literary advertising," Richler switched his main character's preferred scotch from Glenlivet to Macallan. Sure enough, shortly after the book was published two cases of Macallan scotch were delivered to his Montreal apartment.

Dedicated to Florence, <u>Solomon Gursky Was Here</u> ranges from the Canadian Arctic to the Prairies; from the Eastern Townships to Montreal; from 19th

century London to present day New York. The title riffs on the "Kilroy was here" graffiti of World War II, while focusing on the "now you see him, now you don't" flamboyant Solomon Gursky. For Moses Berger who is writing a Gursky family history, Solomon is muse, voice of wisdom, and beloved surrogate father. While the various Gurskys—with the exception of Solomon and his grandfather, Ephraim—are mockingly based on Peter Newman's <u>The Bronfman Dynasty</u>, Newman's book is nowhere mentioned in Richler's list of sources.

1993
Richler had surgery for removal of a polyp.

1995
A news clip in *The Toronto Star* announced that Mordecai Richler had chosen Michael Coren (author of biographies of G. K. Chesterton, H. G. Wells and C. S. Lewis) to write his biography. This was a surprise to everyone who knew of Richler's aversion to anyone other than himself messing with the story of his life.

1997
Richler's tenth novel *Barney's Version* was published by Alfred Knopf, Canada, winning the Giller Prize and Stephen Leacock Award for Humor. The book was dedicated to Florence and "in memory of four absent friends." Richler was now sixty-six years old.

<u>Barney's Version</u> takes place in Montreal, the Eastern Townships, London, and Paris. The fictional Barney is writing his memoirs to blindside the fictional Terry McIver, a fellow expatriate with Barney in the Paris days of their youth. Terry is planning to write his own autobiography in which Barney will be shown in a bad light. <u>Barney's Version</u> is therefore written as an attempt to "set the record straight." Like Richler's seventh novel <u>Joshua Then and Now</u>, <u>Barney's Version</u> begins with the main character in a dismal state: his wife has left him for a younger man, his memory is failing, and his health is in decline. Unlike Joshua in the earlier book (written when Richler was only forty-nine,)

Barney is sixty-seven, and never regains what he has lost. But until the last part of the novel, Barney is vigorously and vengefully engaged in telling the story of his tumultuous three marriages and the colorful pageantry of his life. In the process of remembering his youth and apologizing for past and present sins, he presents himself in as dark a light as the most malevolent biographer might have done.

1998
Richler became a columnist for the *National Post*—a fitting reprise of his first job as reporter for the now defunct *Montreal Herald*. At the age of sixty-eight, he had a cancerous kidney removed at the Montreal General Hospital. While still in hospital, he received a threat on his life because of articles he wrote against the separatist governments of Jacques Parizeau and Lucien Bouchard.

2000
Richler was named a Companion of the Order of Canada.

2001
Mordecai Richler died at the age of seventy from complications following treatment for cancer in his remaining kidney. News of Richler's death, and praise for his contribution to Canadian literature, appeared on the front pages of newspapers across Canada. He was equally commemorated in England and the United States. Among the glowing tributes, Richler's own summing up of his achievements strikes the deepest chord: "I've had a wonderful life. I love my wife. I have wonderful children, and I'm good at my work." Who among us could ask for more than that?

The Acrobats: A Mocking Salute

> *But tell me, who are they, these travelers,*
> *Even a little more fleeting than we ourselves,—*
> *so urgently ever since childhood*
> *wrung by an (oh for the sake of whom?)*
> *never contented will? That keeps on wringing them,*
> *bending them, slinging them, swinging them,*
> *throwing them and catching them back, as though*
> *from an oily smoother air, they come down on the*
> *threadbare carpet, thinned by their everlasting*
> *upspringing, this carpet forlornly*
> *lost in the cosmos.*
> (Rainer Maria Rilke, "Fifth Duino Elegy")

Inspired by Picasso's circus paintings, the poet Rilke created a word-portrait of acrobats driven by an inner restlessness, moving energetically about but getting nowhere. Their efforts are futile because their "carpet"—the ground of their being—is "lost in the cosmos." They are forlorn and bewildered because they have no place to stand.

In Richler's first novel *The Acrobats* we find the same bewildered lost souls, leaping about without knowing why—driven to take a stand without knowing what they are standing for. But unlike Rilke's Elegy which laments the forlorn, restless acrobats, Richler's novel is an acrobatic exercise in itself. It is a mocking high wire act that parodies famous writers of the "lost generation" while telling a sad story of its own. In this novel Richler himself becomes an acrobat as he walks the tightrope of a plausible story-line while tossing in the air literary allusions that keep the reader off balance. What was missed at the time of its publication was that *The Acro-*

bats should be taken as a playful exercise on a serious theme. As the wise old man in the novel explains in another context, it is a "Jewish Joke." This wise old man—called "Chaim" which means "life" in Yiddish—represents the moral center of *The Acrobats*, and the joke he tells is enigmatic at first.

> "When a person is in a state of apprehension and cannot make out the cause of it...what should he do? Let him jump where he is standing four cubits, or let him repeat, 'Hear O Israel, etc': or if the place be unfit for repetition of scripture let him utter to himself, 'the goat at the butcher is fatter than me!' A Jewish joke, you understand."(*Acrobats*, 33)

The point of Chaim's "goat at the butcher" joke, and the reason he suggests that reminding oneself of this joke will lessen one's anxiety, is that the goat—although fat—has been slaughtered for food, while the man—although thin and apprehensive—is not scheduled to die, at least not yet. Since Chaim is an elderly Jew, traveling without a passport and conducting a business on the borderline of legality, his continued survival and ongoing good nature become a triumph of life over adversity. The joke summarizes his wholesome attitude.

But Chaim is not the central character in *The Acrobats*: the main character is Andre Bennet, who functions as the most outrageous Jewish joke that Richler palms off on his readers. Andre is the ultimate suffering hero, carrying a weight of guilt for sins that are not his. The woman he loves says of him, "He has no skin, only blood.... He wants to bleed for everybody." A young couple called Maria and Pepe (Spanish for Mary and Joseph) treat Andre as their son. Of his own parents Andre says, "My father...isn't sure that I'm his son. He thinks I might be the son of a guy named Serge." Andre's friends include thieves, pimps, prostitutes and other outcasts from society. He is killed on a day dedicated to the expiation of sin and laid naked in a cave, his clothes divided up among the men who watched him die. After death he achieves an ironic form of resurrection. Unlike Christ, who rose on the third day after being crucified and appeared to His followers in his usual face and form, Andre is "reborn" as the son of Toni (the woman he loved) and her Nazi lover Kraus. The child has Kraus's face but bears Andre's name.

Early critics of *The Acrobats* did not understand Richler's Jewish joke. They took the novel seriously and faulted it as a serious novel. Because the scope and intent of Richler's enterprise was not clear to readers, and because his story buckled under its literary freight, the book (published in 1954) went rapidly out of print and was for a long time very difficult to find. With Richler's death, and with renewed interest in all his writing, this strange little book—like Andre himself—seems to have been resurrected.

By attributing Christ-like attributes to Andre and undercutting them with savage irony, Richler not only questions the whole concept of Christ as the "Son of God, redeemer of mankind," but also mocks a literary tendency that considers certain types of suffering young men to be Christ figures. Moreover Andre's story is set in the Spanish city Valencia during the *Fiesta de San Jose*: the Festival of St. Joseph who is patron saint of fathers and carpenters. In the light of Andre's confusion about his own actual father, and the tradition that Joseph, husband of Mary, is not really Jesus's father because Jesus is actually the Son of God, this festival is ironic even without Richler's giving it his special spin.

Part Christ-figure and part confused unhappy young man, Andre is also a painter who disclaims his craft:

> As a matter of fact," Andre said, "I'm not a painter at all. I came here to study life in its entirely. One day I hope to write a book about it. You know, like that Who do the bells toll for...Meanwhile I make ends meet peddling hashish at convent doors."(12)

In Andre's joking reference to Hemingway's novel *For Whom The Bell Tolls*, Richler conflates himself with Andre; signals that *The Acrobats* owes a stylistic debt to Hemingway; and ironically distances himself from the master novelist at the same time. Andre's comment that he peddles hashish to nuns to "make ends meet," mocks the situation of impoverished young writers like Richler—not Andre who is described in the story as rich. The hashish part of course questions the morality of Spanish nuns. Since parody can "range from respectful admiration to biting ridicule" (Hutcheon, 15), Richler bathes his characters in a haunting nostalgic glow borrowed from Hemingway and the "lost generation" writers; but in the next breath he dispels the nostalgia with a cold spray of irreverent wit.

Following Hemingway by setting his novel in a Spanish city filled with lost and lonely souls, Richler connects with yet another of his literary heroes by writing a prose summary of W.H. Auden's haunting poem: "O Who Can Ever Gaze his Fill?." Auden's lines draw a bitter-sweet contrast between what men yearn for—a simple life of honest toil; joy in nature's beauty; enduring passionate love; and knowledge that one's sins are all forgiven—and what life actually delivers—failure of crops; malice in strangers; betrayal by lovers and friends. Each stanza contends that life is a cheat and "Not to be born is the best for man." Each stanza except the last admonishes: "Dance while you can." The last stanza wrings a final drop of bitterness out of the tradition that Life is a Dance:

> *The desires of the heart are as crooked as corkscrews*
> *Not to be born is the best for man*
> *The second best is a formal order*
> *The dance's pattern, dance while you can*
> *Dance, dance, for the figure is easy*
> *the tune is catching and will not stop*
> *Dance till the stars come down with the rafters*
> *Dance, dance, dance till you drop*
> ("September 1936")

Richler's prose version preserves the poem's longing for simple pleasures: a longing which contrasts harshly with the bitter conviction that life is a cheat and death is the biggest cheat of all. His prose passage paints a last night of drunken dancing in Valencia before the Festival ends with the *Dia de San Jose*—the Day of St. Joseph when *fallas* (sin offerings) are set on fire in a carnival of exploding lights.

> *They danced until their bodies ached from excess of pleasure (and they thought the earth had fallen out of the sky). They danced until their eyes were swollen with need of sleep (and they saw the buildings were of gold and the streets of soft silk and the lampposts lit by glowing diamonds). They danced until they were too drunk to stand (and they believed the sun was hot and the earth was friendly and the grass was green in spring). They danced until Sunday's dawn filled the sky gloomily and without promise (and they believed in the day and God and they were no longer afraid.)*

Richler's way of separating his "real" world of Valencia from the drunken dancers' wistful belief is by putting what they believe in parentheses: "They danced until Sunday's dawn filled the sky gloomily and without promise (and they believed in the day and God and they were no longer afraid.)" In spite of the parentheses and because of the innate power of words, Richler's version—"And they were no longer afraid"—comes out as more hopeful than Auden's final line—"Dance, dance, dance till you drop." Richler challenges Auden's pessimism by way of parody. Although the prose version lacks Auden's rhythmic beat and the utter perfection of the way he balances idealistic hope against the cynical crushing of hope, Richler, in his own small way and as an utter beginner, is saying, "Here I am, and I can do it too!"

Early on in the novel, Andre's friend Chaim suggests that there are three things a person can do to relieve a state of unendurable anxiety. He can engage in acrobatic activity; he can pray to his God; or he can comfort himself by noting that others are in worse shape than himself. "Let him jump where he is standing four cubits, or let him repeat, 'Hear O Israel, etc.': or if the place be unfit for repetition of scripture let him utter to himself, 'The goat at the butcher is fatter than me!' A Jewish joke, you understand." In Richler's paraphrase of Auden's poem, he invokes dancing as an acrobatic activity that relieves anxiety. In *The Acrobats* as a whole, he follows all three of Chaim's recommendations. He struts across the high wire of his story while tossing his literary borrowings in the air; he affirms his religious heritage by looking at the world and its offers of salvation through "Jewish eyes"; and he provides a context for his protagonist Andre Bennet that shows he is not as badly off as the protagonist of a famous novel by another writer he admires—Malcolm Lowry's *Under the Volcano* (1947).

Richler's "imitation" of *Under the Volcano* is pervasive, but especially marked toward the end of *The Acrobats* when Andre wanders through the streets and bars of Valencia in a drunken, hallucinating stupor. His wanderings lead him directly into the path of the Nazi Kraus, who loves Toni and sleeps with her even though she is engaged to Andre who plans to take her back to Canada. Kraus is brutal, not too bright, and bursting with jealousy because Toni makes it clear that she is sleeping with him more out of pity than love.

The festival of *San Jose* that backgrounds Richler's story of faithless confused lovers is celebrated in Valencia for a week. By night there is drinking and dancing in the street; by day the people construct floats carrying giant wood and *papier mache* figures filled with firecrackers, called *fallas*. At the end of the week the festival culminates in the *Dia de San Jose—the Day of Saint Joseph* when the *fallas* are set on fire, exploding and burning in the night sky, and the people dance wildly as their sins are exploded away. It is on the Day of St. Joseph, while *fallas* explode in the sky, that Kraus and a drunken Andre meet on the bridge. Kraus punches Andre who laughs; so the bigger, stronger Kraus picks him up and throws him off the bridge to die on the rocks below.

Richler's story of an emotionally distraught, good hearted but guilt ridden man wandering through Valencia in a drunken stupor on a religious holiday, until he is killed by his sworn enemy, is Richler's parody of Malcolm Lowry's *Under the Volcano*. Published eight years before *The Acrobats*, Lowry's novel tells the story of Jeffrey Firmin—the Consul of a small Mexican town—who wanders from *cantina* to *cantina* getting progressively more drunk and demented until he is shot and killed by the corrupt Mexican police who throw his body into the *barranca*, a steep ravine that cuts through the town. His death takes place on All Saints Day (November 1st), celebrated in Mexico as "The Day of the Dead," when it is believed that the dead return to their families for one day.

Because Lowry is one of Richler's literary heroes, Richler pays homage to Lowry by imitating him in *The Acrobats*, planting deliberate clues to alert the reader to what he is doing. Near the beginning of *Under the Volcano*, a disembodied voice suddenly booms from a loudspeaker at the railway station: "A corpse will be transported by express." Toward the middle of *The Acrobats,* a disembodied voice proclaims: "The corpse will have to be shipped back to America for Mama." In each novel this voice foretells the hero's fate. But the voice in *Volcano* blaring out of a loudspeaker has a practical purpose and strikes a chilling note, while the voice in *The Acrobats* comes out of nowhere and is mainly meant to remind us of Andre's symbolic role as suffering son. It is at the same time a tag line that connects Richler's story with the one he parodies.

While Andre and the Consul's life stories are quite different, the two men share some startling similarities. Each man nurses the sorrow of an action in the past that poisons any happiness he might claim in his present life. Each has strongly ambivalent feelings about the woman he loves, whom he is supposedly trying to find as he runs to his death. Each is taken to a prostitute's room in his last remaining hours, where he inexplicably showers her with money—an event that somehow seals his fate. Both Andre and the Consul dream of returning to Canada to start a new life. Both drink compulsively to the point of delirium and hallucination, relentlessly destroying themselves, running headlong into death. Both have a moment of clarity and happiness a short time before they die.

> [The Consul] laughed once more, feeling a strange release, almost a sense of attainment. His mind was clear. Physically he seemed better too....He felt free to devour what remained of his life in peace. At the same time a certain gruesome gaiety was creeping into this mood, and, in an extraordinary way, a certain light headed mischievousness. (Volcano, 534)

In *The Acrobats,* Andre has a similar moment of clarity, just before his final, fatal fight with Kraus:

> He walked across to the bridge, still feeling puzzled about some things but richly resolved about others. The bridge, the dead river, the madly lit sky, all seemed wonderfully good....His laugh began slowly, then swelled up and broke out happily. He was not yet certain what was happening to him. It will take time, he thought....Andre laughed again. (*Acrobats*, 204)

A momentary intrusion of happiness before the final catastrophe functions in both novels like the fourth act of a five act Tragic play. In the fourth act we feel that things might work out after all; then in the fifth act the full force of Tragedy is renewed. The Police Chief shoots the Consul and throws his body into the *barranca;*. Kraus beats up Andre and tosses his body over the side of the bridge onto the rocks below. While Andre lies dying under the bridge, Toni, in another part of town watches with wonder as a giant *falla* explodes against the dark night sky. As the Consul falls into the abyss, his wife Yvonne who has been trying to follow him, sees a riderless horse outlined by a sudden flash of lightning, a horse the Consul had cut loose just moments before his death, the horse that will trample Yvonne to death a few minutes later. In keeping with Richler's "imitation with a difference," Toni lives to love again: this time a nice clean-cut American who does not suffer from guilt and who will, presumably, make her happy.

At first sight the festivals that background *The Acrobats* and *Under the Volcano* seem to be different. *El Dia de San Jose* in Valencia celebrates the earthly father of Christ and serves for the expiation of sin. *El Dia de los Muertos*—the Day of the Dead—in Mexico compares to our Halloween where ghosts and goblins are all that remain of the belief that the dead—once a year—return. However, at intervals in *Under the Volcano* a voice asks: *"Quiere usted la salvacion de Mexico? Quiere usted que Cristo sea nuestro Rey?"* (Do you wish the salvation of Mexico? Do you wish Christ to be our King?) The answer always comes back in English: "No!" Richler takes Lowry's theme of salvation refused and damnation enthusiastically embraced, and writes his own version of the story. He creates a troubled, hard-drinking, basically decent young man who, like himself, is adrift in Spain trying to figure out what he is looking for. Andre—because he is patterned on Lowry's death-driven Consul—doesn't survive. But Richler, because he is an acrobat and parodist, thrives on the very things that bring Andre down. He lives to write another day, and another, and another until at last he writes *Barney's Version* and then his novel writing is done.

Under the Volcano is a gorgeous, glorious, funny, ferocious, tragic celebration of drinking oneself to death. It is Malcolm Lowry's masterpiece and the only really good thing he wrote. *The Acrobats* is an apprentice novel that dares to parody the work of literary giants, not coming near them in literary merit, but pulling off some amazing stunts along the way. Eventually Richler's acts of parody will ensure him his own special place among the great writers he dared to imitate in his apprentice work.

Son of a Smaller Hero: Before the Deluge

And the Lord saw that the wickedness of man was great in the earth, and that every imagination of the thoughts of his heart was only evil continually. And it repented the Lord that he had made man on the earth, and it grieved Him to the heart. And the Lord said: I will blot out man whom I have created from the face of the earth; both man and beast, and creeping thing, and fowl of the air; for it repenteth me that I have made them, But Noah found grace in the eyes of the Lord. (Genesis 6:4-8)

Parody, therefore, is a form of imitation, but imitation characterized by ironic inversion, not always at the expense of the parodied text. (Linda Hutcheon, *A Theory of Parody*, 6)

Parody is rampant in *Son of a Smaller Hero*—Richler's "Noah and the Ark" novel—as is autobiography although Richler strenuously denied it. The Bible story describes God's disgust with the wickedness of mankind and His decision to destroy everything He had made by flooding the earth. But because Noah was a righteous man he and his family were saved. Also saved from extinction were pairs of animals, birds, and crawling things that would be needed to replenish the land. Noah is commanded to build an ark that would house his family and the designated creatures. He does as commanded; the waters rise; and the ark moves off.

All flesh perished that moved upon the earth, both fowl and cattle and beast,...and every man...whatsoever was on dry land died....Noah only was left, and they that were with him in the ark. (Genesis 7:21-23)

When the waters finally abate and dry land again appears, Noah leaves the ark; plants a vineyard; and proceeds to get drunk. In his drunken state he is discovered lying "uncovered" in his tent. His youngest son sees Noah naked, and calls the other two brothers who avert their faces, walking backwards into the tent to cover their father with a blanket. Therefore Noah curses the youngest son for lack of respect, but blesses the other two.

In *Son of a Smaller Hero*, the protagonist is called Noah Adler, and his righteousness consists mainly in not telling lies—either to himself or to others—a quality in this story that is his alone. There is no God in *Son of a Smaller Hero*, but there is a kindly, well meaning, impotent man named "Theo": which means "God" in Greek. The flood enters the story only through metaphors, but metaphorically all the unworthy people drown and only Noah is saved. At the end of the novel he sails away, leaving everyone else behind. Noah Adler drinks more than anyone else in Richler's story, and his uncle calls him a drunkard, telling him that he deserves to drown. This is Richler having fun with his sources, since the biblical Noah was saved in spite of a weakness for the fruit of the vine.

In Richler's Noah story, the title's "Smaller Hero" is not Noah Adler, but his meek, self-effacing father ironically named "Wolf." Names are particularly ironic in this novel because they sometimes suggest the opposite of what the characters really are. Noah's grandfather—who has lost the power he once had over his children and grandchildren—is grandly named "Melech" which means "King," as in the opening words to Hebrew prayers: "Blessed art thou O Lord our God, King of the universe." Theo, as already noted, has the Greek name for God without having any God-like characteristics. His name, however, provides a thematic link to the epigraph of Richler's novel (taken from Dostoyevsky's *The Brothers Karamazov):* "If God did not exist, everything would be lawful." In a story that parodies the biblical text in which God decrees the destruction of the world, questions concerning God's existence, non-existence, or possible impotence are not to be dismissed. Along with these larger questions lurking in the background of the story, the smaller hero's major feat invites questions of its own.

In a life of subjugation to his father in whose scrap yard he labors, and in a miserable marriage to a wife he invariably fails to please, Wolf Adler's one act of heroism is to save what he believes to be his father's cash box when the company office at the scrap yard is set on fire. He does not know that the box actually contains his authoritarian father's secret correspondence with a woman he had loved when he was young; nor does he know that these letters are hidden under a number of small Torah scrolls laboriously copied out by hand. When Wolf's body is brought out from the rubble under which it was buried, the people who have gathered around see only Torah scrolls in the box and Wolf is proclaimed a hero who died for the Torah. What no one knows is that Noah—who had jumped into the pit where his father lay buried to protect the body from being mutilated by the crane that was digging him out—had opened the box and taken out the incriminating letters. By this act Noah saves his grandfather's reputation, symbolically covering his nakedness as the good sons in the biblical Noah story covered their father's nakedness with a blanket. And even the blanket makes an appearance in the scene, although not held by Noah.

> *Wolf was huddled up and held an iron box to his stomach. A charred wooden beam was pressed against his back. His face was distorted...his clothes were burned but his body was intact....*
> *Noah turned away but his path was blocked by the stretcher-bearers. His father's body was covered with a blanket.* (159; 161)

The biblical echoes bob along quietly under the surface of a father-son relationship that reveals the son's tenderness, anxiety, and concern. In this novel it is the righteousness of Noah Adler—a son and not a father as in the Bible story—that is emphasized. And it will be Noah Adler's inherent goodness, shown by respect and concern for his father and grandfather, to the point of withholding the truth when it would be hurtful, that gives him the right eventually to sail away. When kindness depends on keeping a secret—which happens again when Noah does not tell his anguished grandfather that it was the grandfather's own youngest son who started the fire—kindness rules. Since the biblical Noah was saved because he was righteous, Noah Adler receives the same reward. However in Richler's secular universe, it is not God who saves Noah, but Noah who must save himself. By spelling out what he considers to be the right behavior, Richler distances himself from a literary source that does not bother to tell us what Noah did to deserve his special fate.

Along with showing why Noah Adler deserves to be saved, Richler indicates through flood and drowning metaphors why his other characters are not worthy. Noah's mother is both unkind and untruthful. She is especially unkind to her husband. When Wolf tries to get away from her endless recriminations by going to the movies, her response is full of sarcasm.

> [Wolf pleads] *'Why can't I do anything right? Do I beat you? I drink? I go with other women?'*
> [Leah scornfully replies] *'Go. Go to the movies. There would be another flood as sure as I'm sitting here if you missed a double feature.'* (36)

When Miriam—who had left her husband so that she and Noah could be together—realizes that Noah's passion is waning, she fears that she will drown.

> *Noah, her lover, had led her out onto the sands and into the water until, having gone so far that it was no longer possible to wade, but necessary to swim, she turned around and saw that the shore was far, far away. What if Noah swam from her?* (127)

Theo, Miriam's husband, cannot face the failure of his marriage and becomes another victim of metaphorical drowning.

> *His eyes filled with the ineffable terror of those who, drowning, search an empty hostile sea for something, anything to hold firm to:*

> *whether that thing be true or not. Nothing's wrong, he thought. I'm tired.* (82)

Theo pretends that nothing is wrong even though he knows that Miriam has left him and is now living with Noah—the young student in his English class whom he had taken home to see his library. Noah, awed by Theo's books and attracted to his beautiful, unsatisfied wife, rejects Theo's proffered friendship and runs away with Miriam. But after a short month of unmarried bliss, Noah begins to cool. Then, when his father dies and his mother tries to drag him back into the Adler cage while at the same time Miriam tugs at him to come back to her, Noah feels that he is drowning too.

> *'Boyele, you won't have to take care of me so long. I probably won't last....'*
> *'Please, Maw, don't talk like that.'*
> *'Your father left an insurance policy of five thousand...'*
> *'Please, don't go on. Please....'*
> *'We can get a small apartment in Outremont.... We...'*
> *The broken oars burst free of their locks. The boat itself broke up underneath him. And Noah, who did not call out for help, felt the waters close over him.*
> *'Yes, Maw. Anything you say.'* (185)

Because "Adler" means "eagle" in Yiddish, Noah Adler—the young eagle—is genetically programmed to leave the nest. And as a righteous man bearing the name of Noah, his biblical destiny is to sail away.

Although Noah's behavior in taking Theo's wife may not be what one would expect from a righteous man, Richler never says that Noah is perfect. His responsibility for the affair is mitigated by his youth and by the older Miriam's obvious dissatisfaction with her husband. She is also painted as promiscuous before her marriage and even more desperately intemperate when she goes back to Theo after Noah leaves. In fact she is shown as drowning in debauchery, her scandalous behavior meticulously clocked by Theo's mother who sits outside her son's bedroom door where a drunken Miriam entertains one lover after another.

> *Mrs. Hall watched the shut bedroom door. She's only been back with him three months, she thought. And that makes the fourth man. She looked at her watch....*
> *Mrs. Hall looked at her watch again. Five minutes, she thought. Why doesn't Theo...*
> *Mrs. Hall looked at her watch. A burst of laughter came from behind the bedroom door.* (219-220)

Why doesn't Theo do something about his wife's behavior? The answer is that he cannot. He can neither help her nor discipline her because he has no power at all: neither for good nor for evil. His inability to act is directly related to his name and Richler's epigraph: "If God did not exist, everything would be lawful." In the fictional world that Theo inhabits, God either does not exist or He has no power. As Wolf is a "smaller hero" so Theo is an impotent god. In Richler's parody of the Noah story people are responsible for their own salvation; and if they cannot save themselves they drown.

Moreover, Theo is not the only failed God in this novel. Theo and his Christian doctrine of love and forgiveness stand in stark contrast to Noah Adler's grandfather, Melech, whose name suggests the Hebrew God of rage and retribution that we see in the Old Testament story of Noah and the Ark—a God who destroys his whole creation in anger at human wickedness. This is the God against whom Richler writes his parody. Here, in Richler's fictional world, the King of the Universe—represented by Melech—is in serious decline.

Richler explores the darker implications of the Noah story while flirting briefly with the alternative God represented by Theo whose God is Love. Noah's short-lived love affair with Miriam is as far as he goes in that direction. The conundrum of the biblical Noah story goes much deeper. Noah was righteous because he "walked with God." But if the God that Noah walked with was an unjust, cruel, vengeful God, what good was there in that walk? And how good a man was Noah himself? Does getting falling down drunk count as righteousness? We learn nothing in the Bible story either about Noah's goodness or about the rest of the world's wickedness. We wonder what Noah's wife, sons, and sons' wives were like. Did they also refrain from wickedness, or were they sinners like everyone else? Why did they get a free ride on the ark? We already know that one of Noah's sons lacked filial respect. And what about Noah's parents? How wicked were they? The Bible is silent, but Richler takes the Bible's silence and re-tells the story in the context of his own life.

As the biblical Noah walks with God, so Noah Adler as a small boy walks with his grandfather Melech. And Melech Adler—when his family is young—does play a kingly role as family patriarch, employer, and enforcer of Talmudic Law. Melech, a rigid disciplinarian, punishes his grandsons when they ignore religious ritual, but sees no harm in cheating Gentile peddlers who bring scrap to his yard. Noah catches him defrauding a peddler, and from then on he cannot walk with Melech. He cannot acknowledge Melech as family king, and he cannot follow the strictures of Melech's God. Noah Adler begins to think for himself and insists on questioning religious laws rather than following them blindly because they are "tradition." This alienates the Adler family, especially his uncle Itzik who condemns Noah in the name of Melech and ritual law:

> *I know more about the laws than any of the boys. Ask Paw. A Jew who doesn't keep the Sabbath isn't worth two cents even. Let my brother, the hero, be a lesson to them. If there's another flood, if...Noah deserves to be dead. Ask Paw.* (169)

Itzik expressly places his nephew Noah in the company of the wicked whom God destroyed in the great flood, condemning him to death for breaking the Sabbath. He has, however, forgotten that the Bible states that it was Noah alone who was saved. Melech is equally convinced that Noah will be punished. But Richler undercuts the old man's self-serving prediction by specifying that it is a God made in his own image on whom Melech depends for justice without mercy.

> *Each man creates God in his own image. Melech's God, who was stern, sometimes just and always without mercy, would reward him and punish the boy. Melech could count on that.* (232)

Son of a Smaller Hero is about a rebellious Noah who breaks with his family's religious rituals because he cannot live with the hypocrisy he sees all around him. Although much of the story is obviously fiction, it has a hard core of biographical fact that gives it power and strength. This core is Richler's own searching for truths he can live by and a way of life he can respect. It is also the recognition that he needs to distance himself from family and community so that he can think straight and fly right.

To validate his own rejection of Jewish tradition and his breaking away from family and Montreal when he sailed for Europe, Richler at first invokes the story of Noah and the Ark—where Noah is commanded by God to save himself, his wife, and his children, allowing the rest of humanity to drown. But in using the Bible story to justify his hero's actions, Richler questions not only the morality of the biblical Noah but also the morality of a God who would destroy his whole creation out of anger with man's wickedness. Surely, being God, He had other options. Noah Adler feels for a time that his options are limited. His sense of honor makes him ask Miriam to marry him even when he knows that he no longer loves her. His relief however is immense when she says no.

Turning away from Miriam and his only experience with Christian love, Noah seeks out his Jewish grandfather one more time and tries to make peace with him. Melech's power was already failing when the novel began, and at the end he has almost no power at all. The children are getting restless. His sons want to take over the yard; his daughter wants to get married; his daughter-in-law, Noah's mother, is disrespectful; and his little brown mouse of a wife bakes raisin buns to keep from facing her family's unhappiness. Noah's disobedience and his flaunting of a non-Jewish mistress cause Melech a secret anguish that Noah only understands after the fire in which his father dies. For when he looks at the things he took from the iron box, he finds letters (written in Polish); receipts for varying amounts of money; and photographs of a plump, blonde, pretty young woman, obviously Gentile, and in some of the pictures holding a child. Noah pieces it all together, realizing that his grandfather had once loved and still longs for a woman forbidden by his strict Orthodox upbringing—a woman with whom he had a child, for whose care he sent support money; a woman to whom he still writes love letters which he "mails" in his iron box. At the time of the fire, Noah only knows that these private letters and pictures must not be made public. Protecting Melech's private life by hiding the evidence of his long ago love affair, Noah leaves behind only the scrolls by virtue of which Wolf is proclaimed a hero. Ironically, Melech had already to some extent "covered himself" by hiding his love letters under religious artifacts—a poignant irony in that it was his religion that forbade his love.

One might think that Melech would have appreciated his grandson's protection, especially when Noah returns the contents of the box and apologizes for not understanding why his grandfather was always so severe. But the old man cannot unbend. He grudgingly gives Noah the scroll he asks for, but will not give him his blessing. In Melech's stark black and white universe, there is no room for any point of view but his own. Having created a God who is "stern, sometimes just, and always without mercy," Melech cannot show either love or mercy himself.

But why—having rejected the rules inscribed in the Torah, and having been rejected by Melech himself—would Noah want the scrolls? Perhaps because he still loved his grandfather and understood the old man's renunciation and pain. Wolf Adler may not have died for the Torah, but Melech had relinquished his only hope of happiness when he abandoned the girl he loved in order to follow the dictates of Torah law. Looking at the letters and photographs made Noah realize that his own desire for Miriam didn't come close to his grandfather's love and loss, and perhaps he wanted the scroll to help him remember that. Even for a secular Jew, the Torah scroll—on which is written the first five books of the Bible—is the most sacred of religious objects: an affirmation of the tradition even for those who do not follow it. Perhaps Noah wanted to keep his grandfather's scroll for the same reason that Richler kept his own father's prayer shawl in a bottom drawer after Moses Isaac Richler died. In a book replete with irony, the final scene between Noah and his grandfather has no irony at all.

> *Melech Adler sat down and picked up his paper again. Their eyes met briefly. An old man crumpled up in a chair.*
> *Noah reached out and touched his shoulder. 'Would you give me one of the scrolls, one of—one of the scrolls you copied...?'*
> *'The scrolls? <u>You.</u> I'm not a scribe...I...'*
> *'I would like to have one to remember—one that you made.'*
> *'They are not very well done, child. There are errors. My father now, he...' Melech got up and opened a drawer. He glanced wordlessly through several scrolls, selected one, and handed it to his grandson.*
> *'I planned so much for you,' Melech began falteringly, 'I...Money you could have had—anything, but....'*
> *'You have given me what I wanted,' Noah said.* (231)

Mordecai Richler never got what he wanted from the grandfather he revered as a child, until he caught the grandfather cheating a Gentile peddler. In later years Richler and his paternal grandfather were completely estranged. Richler also became estranged from his mother, although she did not suffer a heart attack when he left for Europe as Noah's mother did.

> *In seven hours she thought, he'll be gone. There's nothing I can do....*
> *Sweat streamed down her face. Her skin turned gray. A gathering fog of yellow lights, and Leah reached up wearily but in vain for a fading, retreating Noah before she was washed back down under many, heavy seas.* (231)

We don't know whether this heart attack actually kills Leah Adler (whatever "actually" means in a work of fiction), but it certainly relates to the metaphorical drowning of those left behind when Noah goes off to Europe. We don't know what wickedness the people in the Bible story displayed to justify their being destroyed. In *Son of a Smaller Hero,* the drowning metaphor applies to Leah after she tries to manipulate her son into giving up his own life in order to take care of her. It applies to Miriam who tries to make Noah responsible for her after she leaves Theo; and it describes Theo's inability to see that his impotence is at least partially the cause of his failed marriage. When Noah briefly gives in to his mother's demands, the waters close over him too. Facing the truth, whether it be pleasant or unpleasant, is high on Richler's salvation list, as is thinking for yourself and taking responsibility for your actions. Knowing that in the process you will sometimes cause pain to others is the sad corollary to his code of ethics.

Richler's attempt to justify his leaving Montreal by using the precedent of Noah and the Ark founders on the question of who is worthy to be saved, and who is wicked enough to drown. By fictionalizing his own dilemma, maintaining the feelings but rewriting many of the facts, he comes to doubt not only the morality of mankind but also the morality and existence of the Hebrew God: quick to destroy but slow to forgive.

In the novels that follow *Son of a Smaller Hero*, Richler continues to question probe and parody in his effort to find truths worth living and dying for. He subjects literary works, including the Bible, to intense scrutiny—re-fashioning familiar stories in a new context to shatter our preconceptions, and to make us re-evaluate ideas and rules of conduct that we long have taken for granted.

A Choice of Enemies: A Bad Choice

No, I am not Prince Hamlet, nor was meant to be;
Am an attendant lord, one that will do
To swell a progress, start a scene or two,
Advise the prince; no doubt an easy tool,
Deferential, glad to be of use,
Politic, cautious, and meticulous;
Full of high sentence, but a bit obtuse;
At times, indeed, almost ridiculous—
Almost, at times, the Fool.

I grow old…I grow old…
I shall wear the bottoms of my trousers rolled.

T.S. Eliot's poem "The Love Song of J. Alfred Prufrock" portrays a self-effacing, high-principled man who cannot connect with life or love, and fears it is now too late to even try. In *A Choice of Enemies,* Richler takes up the challenge of presenting a type of Prufrock in the day-to-day life situation of a full-length novel. Norman Price, a thirty-eight year old Canadian film writer living in England, is not made of heroic stuff, but he is a good man: cautious, meticulous, high-principled and unable to cope with onslaughts of emotion. Whether it be passion, anger, jealousy, or guilt, Norman runs away rather than staying to work things out. Either he runs out of town to put physical distance between himself and the potentially explosive situation, or he lapses into a state of amnesia. By the time he returns, the feelings will have dissipated or the situation will have resolved without his having to act. Along the way he loses everyone he cares about.

Prufrock, at the end of Eliot's poem, wistfully watches the mermaids singing to each other but not to him, and the reader wistfully watches with him, feeling sweetly nostalgic and enchanted by the delicate images the poetry evokes. Norman Price, being a parody of Prufrock, has no nostalgic wrappings. Norman is every bit as deserving of happiness as Prufrock, and his situation is every bit as sad. But Richler's attitude toward the kind of man Prufrock represents diverges sharply from Eliot's empathy. So Richler plays out Norman's constricted existence against the easy opportunism of a second main character, Ernst Haupt, whose fate comes from a second literary source that Richler parodies. Because our sympathies are divided between two main characters, we do not get too caught up in Norman's sorrows.

When the story begins, Norman has just met Sally, an attractive young American of refreshing frankness and spontaneity. They fall in love, but Norman bungles their first attempt at making love and never tries again.

> *Norman slept on the sofa in his little study, and there, he remembered Sally's freshly washed smell. He recalled her wild blonde hair—the creamy smile—and all at once he felt foolish. He had made an unsuccessful pass at the sweetheart of the Sigma Something. No more.*
> ....
> *Norman, after the first night's failure, had shied away from trying to make love to her again. He lived in perpetual fear of rejection.*
> (38,41)

By shying away from another lovemaking attempt, by accepting his first failure as his fate, Norman imitates Prufrock, but with a difference.

> *Should I, after tea and cakes and ices,*
> *Have the strength to force the moment to its crisis?*
> ....
> *I have seen the moment of my greatness flicker,*

> *And I have seen the eternal Footman hold my coat and snicker,*
> *And in short, I was afraid.* ("Prufrock," lines 79-87)

The magic of Eliot's poetry arouses our compassion in a way that Richler's prose version flatly refuses to do. Norman downgrades his lovemaking failure to an "an unsuccessful pass." But Prufrock acknowledges the magnitude of his defeat: "I have seen the moment of my greatness flicker,/And I have seen the eternal Footman hold my coat and snicker,/and in short, I was afraid." Where Prufrock accepts his state as sadly definitive, Norman brushes it—and Sally—aside as of no consequence, even though he is now afraid to try again.

In contrast to Norman and his Prufrockian timidity, Richler adds to the story a young, handsome, energetic, unscrupulous East German refugee recently arrived in London—Ernst Haupt. The moment we realize that "Ernst Haupt" is a loose Germanized translation of *The Importance of Being Earnest*, another layer is added to the parody. Richler's title, *A Choice of Enemies*, comes from a line in Oscar Wilde's *The Picture of Dorian Gray* (a borrowing first pointed out by literary critic George Woodcock). Now Richler wittily inverts two German words—*haupt* from *hauptsache* which means "the main thing" and *ernst* which means "earnest"—to approximate the title of Wilde's witty romantic comedy *The Importance of Being Earnest*. Since Ernst Haupt's eruption into Norman's life changes that life irrevocably, Ernst's behavior to a large extent drives the plot.

"A man cannot be too careful in the choice of his enemies," proclaims Lord Henry Wotton in *The Picture of Dorian Gray*—as he corrupts the young Dorian. A man must be very careful in the title of his books and the naming of his characters, would be Richler's response as he fashions a protagonist who is already corrupt, but in an engaging sort of way.

However, Ernst Haupt's role in Richler's novel is more complicated than simply being the handsome rogue who steals Norman Price's "sweetheart of the Sigma Something." The underlying situation is that Norman receives news that his younger brother Nicky has been killed in Germany. Unable to cope with his brother's death, his frustrated passion for Sally, and his fear that she will reject any further advances from him, Norman bolts. He leaves London for Europe and ends up on the island of Ibiza. While he is away, Sally—to whom he has not even said goodbye or given any reason for his flight—meets Ernst Haupt. She is lonely and feeling rejected. He is lonely and arrogant. They fall into bed and in love. By the time Norman returns to London, emboldened by a successful encounter with a lusty American girl, he is ready to try Sally again. Indeed he is ready to ask her to marry him. However by now she is totally involved with Ernst, and does not even notice Norman's readiness. Having pumped himself up to propose, only to learn that his proposal is no longer relevant, Norman has a supremely Prufrockian moment:

> *Norman wiped his graying curly hair with a clammy hand. He lit a cigarette. Looking at Sally again he saw her briefly as a shallow young girl intent on thrills; no more. But the impression didn't last long enough to help him. Suppressing an urge to toss them both out of the room, Norman poured tea.* (65)

He consoles himself with the thought that had he proposed and been accepted, "It wouldn't have worked out anyway."(67). Norman's bringing himself to the point of asking an "overwhelming question"—in the context of pouring tea—and then, having not asked the question, wondering whether it would have been worth the effort, is a prose summary of Prufrock's existential dilemma.

> *And would it have been worth it after all,*
> *After the cups, the marmalade, the tea,*
> *Among the porcelain, among some talk of you and me,*
> *Would it have been worth while,*
> *To have bitten off the matter with a smile,*
> *To have squeezed the universe into a ball*
> *To roll it toward some overwhelming question,*

> To say: 'I am Lazarus, come back from the dead,
> Come back to tell you all'—
> If one, settling a pillow by her head,
>   Should say: 'that is not what I meant at all.
>   That is not it at all.' ("Prufrock," lines 88-99)

Norman tolerates Sally's affair with Ernst and even tries to befriend the young man, to the point that he alienates his own old friends who are not willing to accept someone they consider a Nazi punk. But then Norman is hit with horrific news. He learns that Ernst is the man who is responsible for his half brother Nicky's death. Since Nicky had a different surname from Norman's (through some complicated situation of having been adopted by an aunt), Ernst has no inkling that he has not only stolen Norman's intended wife, but also killed his brother. When Ernst finds out what he has done, he flees to Canada. Sally, left alone again, tries to persuade yet another man to take her more seriously, by pretending to commit suicide. The man doesn't come in time to rescue her, and Sally dies.

This piling on of coincidence was judged harshly by reviewers of Richler's novel. It was considered a gross error in story telling, "comparable [in one reviewer's words] to some out-dated Jacobean Tragedy." What the critics did not realize was that Richler had gone back further than the Jacobeans—all the way to Greek Tragedy—and was writing a modern parody of Sophocles' play, *Oedipus Rex*. Not only that, but toward the end of Richler's novel Ernst gets involved in a second parody of the Oedipus legend: this time with one crucial fact reversed. In the first parody Ernst unknowingly kills Norman's half-brother and then almost marries Norman's hoped-for wife. In the second parody Ernst saves an old man from death (in *Oedipus Rex* the old man is killed), and then an older woman whose husband's identity papers Ernst has bought insists that he must marry her.

The well-known Tragedy of Oedipus is the story of a man who cannot outrun his fate. When he is born, his parents—the King and Queen of

Thebes—are warned by an oracle that their son is destined to kill his father and marry his mother. Although they hand the baby boy to a shepherd telling him to expose the infant on a hillside where he will die, the shepherd gives Oedipus to another couple who bring him up as their own. Again an oracle intervenes and warns Oedipus that he will kill his father and marry his mother. He therefore runs away from his foster parents (thinking that they are his real parents), to avoid doing them harm. He travels to the city of Thebes and, at a crossroads, kills an old man who threatens him from a passing carriage. Arriving in Thebes, he answers the riddle of the Sphinx who had been holding the city in thrall, and is rewarded by marriage to the recently widowed Queen. A plague falls on the city; Oedipus seeks out seers to learn the cause; and eventually learns that he himself is the cause: because the man he killed was his father and the Queen he married was his mother. The play ends with Jocasta, his mother and wife, committing suicide and Oedipus plucking out his eyes. The city then recovers from the plague and the blind Oedipus wanders off.

Richler does not write tragic novels: he writes parody. He does not write poetry either, which is why he makes his Prufrockian hero so prosaic. In Richler's parody, he makes the tragedy first incomplete and then to some extent inverted. As Oedipus, Ernst is forced to fight with Norman's half-brother who rushes toward him with a broken beer bottle. Ernst kills him purely in self-defense. He then beds Norman's intended wife not knowing Norman's intentions. Later, when Ernst—after finding out what he has done—runs away to Canada, he reenacts the Oedipus story with a difference. He buys the identity papers of an unattractive older woman's dead husband after saving an old man from being crushed by a collapsing wall. Landing in hospital with a broken leg, Ernst desperately tries to avoid being claimed in marriage by the woman whose husband's papers he has bought. The identity papers that seal Ernst's fate relate back to the Sphinx's riddle that Oedipus had solved in the original story: What walks on four legs in the morning? On two legs at noon? And on three legs at night? The answer is "Man" who crawls as a baby, walks upright in his prime and requires a cane in old age. By buying another man's identity papers Ernst legally becomes a different man. By breaking his leg he is also—like Oedipus—maimed. The sphinx's riddle is considered to be the existential question: what is a man? Richler changes the context by raising the question: who are you when you acquire someone else's identity and marry his wife?

Back home in London, Sally—who is no longer any man's wife or intended wife—kills herself in despair. When last seen, Ernst Haupt—with his broken leg in traction—vainly struggles to escape his unwanted future bride's embrace. The point of playing the story twice and inverting it the second time where the hero saves an old man instead of killing him, and then tries unavailingly to refuse his wifely "reward," is to turn what is often considered the world's most perfect tragedy into pure farce. Neither of Richler's protagonists dies at the end of the story: Norman gets married by default; Ernst gets engaged against his will. Both will probably live unhappily ever after.

While Ernst plays out his second Oedipal parody, Norman goes back to playing Prufrock and running away from reality. After he learns that it is Ernst who killed his half-brother, Norman slides into amnesia for the second time in his life. In his wandering amnesic state he meets a woman named Vivian, whom he does not particularly care for but whose kindness he accepts. Although he sleeps with her, he is in fact totally indifferent. At this point we remember the speech in Oscar Wilde's *The Picture of Dorian Gray*, from which Richler took the title of his novel.

> "You don't understand what friendship is, Harry," he murmured—"or what enmity is, for that matter. You like every one; that is to say, you are indifferent to every one." "How horribly unjust of you!" cried Lord Henry....I make a great difference between people. I choose my friends for their good looks, my acquaintants for their good characters, and my enemies for their good intellects. A man cannot be too careful in the choice of his enemies."(*The Picture of Dorian Gray*, 19)

Wilde's ironic cynicism obviously appealed to Richler since Norman, the primary protagonist of *A Choice of Enemies,* is extremely careless in his choice of friends and enemies. At the end of the novel he is manipulated into marrying a woman who has neither good character, good looks, nor intelligence to commend her.

> *After Norman had walked Vivian back to the basement flat on Oakley Street she invited him inside for a nightcap…So this, he thought, is as good a time as any to tell her that I'm leaving the country.*
> *'I think we'd better stop seeing each other,' Vivian said suddenly.*
> *'Why?'*
> *'You feel obligated to me because I took care of you while you were ill.'…*
> *'So,' She continued in an edgy voice, 'I think it would be better if we didn't see each other again.'*
> *Norman fiddled anxiously with his glasses. 'Would you like to marry me?' he asked.*
> *………………………………………………………………*
> *Norman kissed her on the mouth. She didn't respond very warmly.*
> (211)

Norman's rash proposal shows that he still cannot look reality in the face. He neither loves Vivian nor finds her sexually attractive; but her reminder that she had looked after him when he suffered from amnesia sends him into a fluster of guilt. Her lack of response to his kiss is an ominous foretaste of marital troubles to come.

Norman's behavior toward Vivian after his second amnesia is markedly different from the way he treats Karp, who looked after him during his first amnesia and is now his landlord. Karp is a Jew, physically unattractive but a good man, and desperate for Norman's affection. In this he resembles another Jew whose friendship Norman spurned when they were fellow pilots in the Second World War. Norman's reason for shying away from his fellow pilot and now from Karp is that both men display "all the unfortunate characteristics the anti-Semite attributes to [their] people"

(34). This suggests that Norman, decent man though he is, is also to some extent anti-Semitic: comfortable only with Jews who do not act "too Jewish." And Richler punishes Norman for this. Karp turns to revenge. He spreads lies about Norman to Norman's old friends and colleagues who have already started turning against him because of the friendship with Ernst. Eventually Norman is isolated from friends and enemies alike, and ends up with Vivian.

Karp finds the first eager audience for his lies in Charlie—an unsuccessful script writer and one of Norman's puzzling choices as a friend. Norman had gone out of his way to help Charlie by re-writing a script that would otherwise have been rejected. When Charlie finds out that it was Norman who had saved his script, he turns viciously against him and joins Karp in depriving Norman of the few friends he still has left. Charlie's behavior recalls one of Oscar Wilde's famous aphorisms: "Let no good deed go unpunished."

Besides lying to Norman's friends, it is Karp who informs Norman that Ernst is responsible for his brother's death in Germany. Not waiting for Norman to recover from hearing that the young man he had befriended at such cost was the one who killed his brother, Karp goes on to slyly suggest that with Ernst removed, Norman and Sally might have another chance. Unable to admit that Karp has read his secret thoughts, Norman turns on him with cold fury: "The best ones were killed, Karp. Only the conniving evil ones like you survived"(146). Since Karp did indeed survive a Nazi concentration camp, no insult could cut more deeply than this. And no statement could show more clearly how Norman Price feels about certain kinds of Jews.

As Richler parodies Oscar Wilde's title *The Importance of Being Earnest* by naming his second protagonist "Ernst Haupt," so he parodies a philosophical statement in Wilde's *The Picture of Dorian Gray* by naming his main character "Norman Price."

> *Each man lived his own life, and paid his own price for living it. The only pity was one had to pay so often for a single fault. One had to pay over and over again, indeed. In her dealings with man Destiny never closed her accounts.* (Dorian Gray, 216)

The "single fault" that Norman has to pay "his own price for" is that he cannot stand "pushy Jews." And by slapping away the hands of friendship he inadvertently makes certain Jews his "choice of enemies." Hence Richler's title and Norman's sad decline.

Both Oscar Wilde's *Picture of Dorian Gray* and Sophocles' *Oedipus Rex* rely heavily on the concept that man cannot outrun his fate. "The Love Song of J. Alfred Prufrock" implies that character is destiny, with Prufrock's fate already implicit in the prudery that his name suggests. Although Ernst Haupt is a likable chap in many ways, Richler does not let us forget that he is a German who was once a member of the Hitler Youth, and who, in Canada, buys the identity papers of a former S.S. Officer. The price he pays for this is that the officer's widow comes with the identity papers no matter how hard Ernst objects. As a further insult—only mentioned on the last page of the book—Ernst has to give up his name along with his freedom since his name must now correspond with the papers he has bought. So Ernst Haupt as we knew him essentially disappears.

The Norman Price we met at the beginning of the book has also pretty well disappeared by the end. He no longer has a job or friends and must make do with the friends of his wife whom he dislikes as much as he is beginning to dislike her. He and Vivian do not agree on anything, and Norman's last wistful thought is that perhaps he and Vivian might invite their attractive upstairs neighbor—a fashion model—to dinner.

> *I shall wear white flannel trousers, and walk upon the beach.*
> *I have heard the mermaids singing each to each.*
>   *I do not think that they will sing to me.*
>   ("Prufrock," lines 125-27)

J. Alfred Prufrock sings his love song into the void; Richler shows us in his novel how the love life of a Prufrockian man might play out. When T.S. Eliot first wrote "The Love Song of J. Alfred Prufrock" he was unattached and studying philosophy at Harvard. But by the time his poem was revised and published in 1917, he had already met and impulsively married Vivian Haigh-Wood, and was sincerely regretting what he had done. When Mordecai Richler wrote *A Choice of Enemies,* he had already disentangled himself from his impulsive, unhappy first marriage, and was contemplating a happier union with the beautiful fashion model, Florence Wood. Richler's first bad marriage becomes the punishment for Norman Price—who waits too long to propose to Sally, and then makes the disastrous choice of marrying Vivian (named after T. S. Eliot's first wife who made him so unhappy). Yet at the very end of his novel, Richler—perhaps contemplating his own happier future—seems to relent: he allows Norman to direct his thoughts toward the attractive model living upstairs.

> *Norman poured himself a stiffer drink. He wondered whether Vivian would object to asking Kate round to dinner tomorrow night.* (*Choice,* 217).

T.S. Eliot also had a second chance at happiness when he married his secretary and had eight contented years before he died.

The Apprenticeship of Duddy Kravitz: A Parody of Success

The first time I saw him he couldn't have been much more than sixteen years old. A little ferret of a kid, sharp and quick...Always ran. Always looked thirsty. (What Makes Sammy Run?, 3)

Duddy Kravitz was a small, narrow-chested boy of fifteen with a thin face. His black eyes were ringed with dark circles and his pale, bony cheeks were crisscrossed with scratches. (The Apprenticeship of Duddy Kravitz, 5)

The Apprenticeship of Duddy Kravitz reminds us of Budd Schulberg's *What Makes Sammy Run?:* in the physical description of the two boys when first they appear on the scene; in their willingness to use fair means and foul to achieve their goals; and in the boundless energy and self-confidence that propels them along. By closely imitating certain aspects of Schulberg's novel, Richler at times skates close to the edge of plagiarism—which he avoids by subverting the story he imitates. Because Sammy Glick is so irredeemably awful, and because he represents a certain kind of reprehensible immigrant to America, Richler presents his Canadian version of Sammy as a more complex human being with a certain amount of goodness and grace. Where Sammy makes his way up the ladder by stealing scripts and stories which he passes off as his own, Duddy's path to success involves the more or less honest acquisition of land.

There's plenty of good, dead authors that'll hand you terrific picture plots on a silver platter. Why, I knew a guy who made a nice little pile out of one of de Maupassant's stories just the other day. And all he had to do was switch the hooker from a French carriage to a Western stagecoach. If you were smart you'd try to hit on something like that and write yourself an original. (*What Makes Sammy Run?* 69)

In Budd Schulberg's story, Sammy was advised by a studio head to write film scripts based on stories by famous dead writers, such as de Maupassant. But Sammy, impatient for success and not a great writer himself, short-circuited the process, hustling his way up the Hollywood ladder by plagiarizing scripts written by his peers. So good was he at stealing the work of other writers that he ended up rich, hated, and alone. Because he believed that "going through life with a conscience [was] like driving your car with the brakes on," Sammy Glick could never understand why he was so disliked or why, despite all his efforts, he never had any fun. As a case study in monstrous egotism, Sammy fascinated Al Manheim, the narrator of Schulberg's book (as he clearly fascinated Mordecai Richler):

> *In Sammy was everything I hated most: dishonesty, officiousness, bullying. But I felt I wasn't only staring at him with dislike, I was staring at him with actual awe for the magnitude of his blustering.* (*Sammy*, 35)

When Richler came to write his parody of *What Makes Sammy Run?* it was surely "the magnitude of [Sammy's] blustering" that first attracted him. And it is the sheer energy with which Duddy Kravitz pursues his goals that most fascinates the reader of Richler's book.

Bud Schulberg tries to account for Sammy's awfulness in his forward to *What Makes Sammy Run?*

> *The ultra-aggressive, ruthless and belligerently self-centered type [is] rather common among second-generation Americans from impoverished immigrant families where the father has lost his prestige due to his inability to cope with his new environment.* (xiii)

He suggests that Sammy Glick is at least partly a victim of cultural conditions. Richler at first seems to follow in Schulberg's track but soon veers off. Duddy's father, Max, boasts that Duddy "was born on the wrong side of the tracks with a rusty spoon in his mouth," but he was "one that thrived on adversity" (375). Max, who is a taxi driver and small-time pimp, does not explain Duddy's ruthlessness by his impoverished background, but rather boasts about what he and Duddy regard as success. This definition of success, of becoming a "Somebody," gives the novel its bite and rivets the reader's attention. Max's idea of a "Somebody" is the local "Boy Wonder," a small-time gangster and drug dealer who hands out jobs and money to people in the neighborhood, one day a week. Crippled by polio and physically repulsive, Jerry Dingleman, the Boy Wonder, is admired partly for the good he does, but mostly for his wealth and power. Max advises Duddy to emulate the Boy Wonder if he wants to get anywhere in life. Duddy's grandfather, on the other hand, categorically states: "a man without land is nothing." Duddy tries to please both his grandfather and his father; but in the process of becoming a "somebody" in his father's eyes, he loses his grandfather's love and respect.

Because parody is a form of imitation that undercuts the similarity between two literary works by stressing critical difference, Richler gives Duddy Kravitz several models on which to fashion his future. Sammy Glick is one model and Jerry Dingleman another. Richler's imitation of *What Makes Sammy Run?* includes Duddy's physical description, his ruthless streak, and the ambiguous advice he receives on how to succeed. Sammy Glick is told to "rip off" famous dead authors, but not warned that ripping off his colleagues is entirely a different matter. Duddy Kravitz accepts that he must own land to become a "Somebody," but only half understands that his grandfather expects him to do it in an honorable way. His grandfather, an upright man, assumes that Duddy is like himself; his father, who uncritically admires the local gangster, has no moral compass to guide his son. However, since the Boy Wonder is not just a drug dealer but also a local benefactor, Duddy absorbs the lesson that a rich, powerful, propertied man should take care of his own people. In this, Richler is already beginning to separate Duddy Kravitz from Sammy Glick, because Sammy cared for, and took care of, no one but himself.

Duddy Kravitz is as clever, energetic, ruthless, and sly as Sammy Glick, but Richler maintains the critical distance that parody demands by adding another aspect to Duddy's nature. And this better part comes from a different literary source. "Duddy" is a Jewish nickname for "David," (pointed out by Michael Greenstein in "The Apprenticeship of Noah Adler," *Canadian Literature*, Autumn 1978). And the biblical David accounts for everything in Duddy that is brave and good. In the Bible, David in his apprenticeship stood up to the giant Philistine bully, Goliath, and killed him with a slingshot and a stone. While still a young man, he played the harp for King Saul, soothing his dark moods with music. Later when the king sought David's life, the young David remained loyal. When David himself became King of the Israelites, he conquered the Philistines and took their land.

Duddy's affectionate and music-loving side, his fighting spirit, and his family loyalty all come from the David side of his heritage. To demonstrate the similarity, Richler parodies the story of "David and Goliath" when Duddy drives the Boy Wonder off his recently acquired land armed only with outrage and a stone.

> *Duddy laughed some more. "Listen, Dingleman," he shouted, "get off my land. Beat it."*
> *"Duddy," Max began, "What's got into you?"*
> *"Take off, Sonny."*
> *Max began to shake Duddy.*
> *"You'll never do it alone," Dingleman said.*
> *Duddy broke free. "I'm giving you five minutes to get the hell off my land. I'm the king of the castle here, Sonny."...*
> *Duddy picked up a stone.* (370)

As David fought winning battles against the large tribes who surrounded his small country, so Duddy battles the French Canadians who would not let a Jew buy land in their midst. But since this is a parody, Duddy's battle with hostile tribes does not involve actual warfare. His trusted French Canadian girlfriend buys the land for him, acting against her own people to help him achieve his dream.

Duddy's land surrounds a pristine mountain lake clearly taken from *What Makes Sammy Run?*—a lake revealed in a scene between Al Manheim the narrator and Kit, the young woman he loves.

> *As we took a hairpin turn Kit said, 'There's my little beach down there.'*
> *I saw nothing but steep rocks below us piling into the water.*
> *She said, 'I found it one hot day driving up to Frisco. It's a beautiful place to go swimming in the raw.'*
> *'Was Sammy ever down here with you?'*
> *She shook her head. 'I pointed it out to him once, but he didn't want to stop. No one ever taught him to relax.'* (Sammy, 188, 189)

In *Duddy Kravitz,* the scene plays out the same way at first. Duddy is brought to a hidden mountain lake by his girlfriend, Yvette.

> *They started up a narrow path over the mountain.*
> *"Jeez. I thought we were going swimming."*
> *"You'll see."...*
> *"The lake's right here," she said.*
> *"Wha?"...*
> *"Go to the top of the hill."*
> *Duddy climbed the rest of the rise....*
> *Before him spread a still blue lake and on the other side a forest of pine trees. There was not one house on the lake....*
> *"Have you ever brought anyone else here before?"...*
> *Duddy realized that they were both nude and for the first time he was embarrassed....*
> *"We used to come here to swim when we were kids."...*
> *"How far is it from the road?"*
> *"About half a mile, maybe more."*

> "Can you see the road from there?"
> "No."...
> He could watch the lake over her shoulder and in his mind's eye it was not only already his but the children's camp and the hotel were already going up. (105-109)

Like the biblical Eve, Yvette is unaware of doing harm. However she tempts Duddy by showing him the beautiful mountain lake where she and her brothers used to swim naked in their innocent youth. When he sees the lake and the land surrounding it, Duddy remembers his grandfather's pronouncement: "A man without land is nothing," and resolves to make this land his own. He breaks free of Yvette's affectionate embrace and races down to the lake where he dives down again and again. When he comes out he realizes that they are both naked, and feels ashamed.

Here Richler once again dips into the Bible—this time to add his own version of Adam's fall from grace to the scene that begins as a borrowing from *What Makes Sammy Run?*. The beautiful lake and surrounding land are paradise, and Yvette's name is diminutive for Eve. Duddy's diving to the bottom of the lake represents Adam's fall, after which he notices for the first time that he and Yvette are naked. And he feels ashamed. By bringing echoes of the fall of mankind to his story of a young man scrambling up the ladder of success, Richler darkens Duddy's first step toward realizing his dream.

Duddy's "Promised Land" has the shape of a beautiful mountain lake and the land that surrounds it. In his mind it immediately becomes the site of a children's camp and a hotel that would belong entirely to him. He knows that he will have to scheme and scrape to obtain this land, but does not know to what depths his efforts will take him.

When Richler wrote this book he also had a Promised Land in mind. In 1960 (the year after *Duddy Kravitz* was published), Richler was finally able to marry Florence—the wife of his friend Stanley Mann. He had wanted her from the moment he saw her (fictionalized in *Barney's Version* as at his own first wedding). He wanted to have a home and children with his beloved Florence, and he signified this in the novel by Duddy's vision of a hotel and children's camp on the land he had already claimed for himself.

Richler, like Duddy, saw where his happiness lay and took it. The unhappiness of his first marriage taught him that a man without the right woman was nothing. This he translated into Duddy's grandfather's mantra: "A man without land is nothing." However, in the process of getting his land Duddy trivialized his relationship with Yvette, and betrayed Virgil's friendship and trust. Richler left his first wife and denigrated her in his novels. To achieve his own happiness, he took the wife of a friend. This was painful for everyone concerned and left Richler with a heavy load of guilt. In novel after novel Richler would give his protagonists the guilt that came with shedding his first wife and winning the woman he loved. Finally in his last novel, *Barney's Version*, he sent an offering to the gods by changing the order of events. Barney, after many years of marriage, lost the woman who was from first to last his heart's desire, to a man he considered more worthy than himself.

Research differs from plagiarism in that borrowed sources are clearly acknowledged. Literary parodies are distinct from "stealing another writer's words or ideas" because the imitations are meant to be noticed. If they are not noticed, then half the fun is gone. Richler alerts us to the fact that *The Apprenticeship of Duddy Kravitz* is based on *What Makes Sammy Run?* by imitating, in his own inimitable way, character descriptions, scenes, and themes from Schulberg's novel. He also specifically invokes his predecessor's book when a school friend calls out to Duddy, "Well look who's here, Sammy Glick"(168). However, in spite of his acknowledgments and the transparency of his imitations, Richler's borrowing characters and scenes from a novel in which the main character made his fortune by stealing the work of other writers is an act of impudence that is hard to beat.

> *Parody can obviously be a whole range of things. It can be serious criticism, not necessarily of the parodied text; it can be playful, genial mockery....Its range of intent is from respectful admiration to biting ridicule. (A Theory of Parody, 15)*

What Makes Sammy Run? was greatly admired when it was published in 1941 and Richler's parody is not meant to ridicule Schulberg's achievement. It is rather a gesture of admiration and respect, giving a Canadian twist to the "young man clawing his way up the ladder" theme. Nor is Richler necessarily mocking the Bible, although his attitude toward Bible stories is always less than reverential. By giving Duddy a divided soul—part scoundrel and part biblical hero—and presenting Duddy's fall from grace as an echo of the fall of mankind, Richler maintains a critical distance from all his sources. At the same time he creates a character so true to life that when the film of this novel was made, more than a few former residents of St. Urbain Street claimed to be the model for Duddy Kravitz.

As a fictional character, Schulberg's Sammy Glick holds our interest at least partly because he is seen through the eyes of the very likable Al Manheim whose story we also follow. In real life, Sammy would be considered scum: someone we would make every effort to avoid. The biblical David as a young man was impossibly good: again and again saving King Saul even when Saul—jealous of David's popularity—tried to have him killed. David was a hero, an ideal to be looked up to, not a human being we could imagine meeting. But when David and Sammy are forged together in Duddy Kravitz, we have a young man we can identify with and understand. So we cringe when he does cruel and vulgar things and cheer when he does well.

While Sammy Glick had only Al Manheim as a friend, Duddy has three people who sincerely love him, and whom he bitterly disappoints: the grandfather who gives him easily misunderstood advice; Yvette who puts up with Duddy's egotism, vulgarity, and inability to care deeply about anyone who is not "family"; and Virgil the epileptic poet who admires Duddy with a puppy dog love, and is crippled because of Duddy's inattention to danger. Virgil and Yvette become touchstones for Duddy's callous disregard for those who are neither family nor Jews. And this is where Richler distances himself most clearly from *What Makes Sammy Run?*. Sammy Glick cheerfully cheated Jew and Gentile alike and had no sense of responsibility or guilt. Our fascination with him results from the sheer awfulness of his behavior and because we wonder whether justice will ever catch up with him—as finally it does.

At the end of *What Makes Sammy Run?* Al Manheim describes the place that Sammy has reached:

> *You're alone, pal, all alone. That's the way you wanted it, that's the way you learned it,...all alone in crowded theaters, company conventions, all alone with twenty of Gladys' girls tying themselves into lewd knots for you. All alone in sickness and in health, for better or worse...'til death parts you from your only friend, your worst enemy, yourself.* (303)

Duddy Kravitz has no Al Manheim to mediate between him and the reader, to tell us how things really are at the end. Having alienated his three strongest supporters Duddy Kravitz would seem to have isolated himself like Sammy Glick. He complains to Yvette when she finally rejects him: "I have to do everything alone. I can see that now. I can trust nobody." But he is not alone in the same way that Sammy is. Even at the end, when Virgil is paralyzed after Duddy hired him to drive his company truck at night—aware that he might have an epileptic attack and crash—Virgil forgives him. He also forgives Duddy for forging Virgil's signature to the cheque that paid for the last parcel of his precious land.

After Duddy's betrayal of Virgil's trust, Yvette wants nothing more to do with the man whose "girl Friday" she had willingly become. Instead she dedicates herself to taking care of the crippled Virgil. Only after she rejects him for the last time does Duddy realize what he has lost. When the grandfather whom he had tried to impress also turns his back, Duddy is crushed. But, having finally become a "Somebody" in the eyes of his foolish, ethically-challenged father, and in the eyes of his father's circle of friends, Duddy momentarily feels triumphant and absolved of guilt, washed clean by his father's admiration. The last words of the novel, ironic though they may be, are happy.

> *And suddenly Duddy did smile. He laughed. He grabbed Max, hugged him, and spun him around. "You see," he said, his voice filled with marvel. "You see." (377)*

We don't know what Max sees, but as readers we see that Duddy's fate is not sealed the way Sammy's was at the end of his story. Duddy still has his double character and therefore still has choices open to him. We also begin to see what Richler has done in this parody of success. The implicit judgment that parody involves is not directed at Schulberg's novel, but at specific faults in the society where Richler grew up—which is why Montreal Jews reacted with outrage. Later when the book became a success, and especially after it was made into a movie, many of his former critics became his fans. Schulberg had stated in the introduction to *What Makes Sammy Run?*:

> *The Sammy-Drive is still to be found everywhere in America, in every field of endeavor and among every racial group. It will survive as long as money, prestige and power are ends in themselves, running wild, unharnessed from usefulness. (x)*

Richler makes no such claim. Duddy's family comes from the same background as Sammy's; but Duddy does not run away from his foolish father the way Sammy does. On the contrary: he runs to win his father's respect and love. The ambiguous ending, where Duddy finally gains his father's esteem while losing the respect of his grandfather and Yvette, gives his vaunted success a bitter twist.

Unlike Schulberg, whose target was the Sammy-drive found in every racial group in America, Richler parodies a specific narrow-mindedness held by certain Jews, especially after the second world war. A Jewish businessman who had befriended Duddy put it this way:

> *A plague on all <u>Goyim</u>, that's my motto. The more money I make the better care I take of my own, the more I'm able to contribute to our hospital, the building of Israel, and other worthy causes. So a <u>goy</u> is crippled and you think you're to blame. Given the chance he would have crippled you,"* he shouted, *"or thrown you into a furnace like six million others. You think I didn't lose relatives? I lost relatives."*... "Jeez," Duddy said, "Wait a minute. Virgie is no nazi." *(311)*

Stunned by the ferocity of his friend, Duddy refuses to believe that this has anything to do with him. He has however diligently practiced what has just been preached.

In the opening pages of the novel, Duddy as a sixteen year old methodically destroys the teacher who dared to criticize his father. When Virgil comes into his life filled with admiration and longing to be of service, Duddy uses him with callous disregard and robs him at the end. In his relationship with Yvette, Duddy (secretly ashamed of loving a chambermaid) allows her to satisfy his lust, run his office, and take care of his land transactions, but shows her no real affection or respect. Only at the end when she turns her back on him does Duddy feel the loss.

But in relation to his family, Duddy shows only loyalty and concern. He rescues his brother Lennie—a first year medical student—from the aftermath of a botched abortion he had foolishly agreed to perform. He loves and protects his foolish father. When the uncle who had always preferred Lennie to Duddy lies dying of cancer, Duddy drags home his uncle's silly, promiscuous wife, insisting she comfort the dying man. The only Jews he fights against are those who have "done him dirt": the haughty society girl who humiliated him; the rich spoiled young man who put her up to it; Jerry Dingleman who refused to lend him money when Duddy was desperate, but tried to become his partner after Duddy had bought his land. Although Duddy does some awful things himself we cheer when those who have hurt him are paid back. But it is the hard-working hard-fighting underdog that we cheer, not the callous egotist. His Uncle Benjy, in a letter that Duddy reads after his uncle's death, puts it all in perspective:

> *There's more to you than mere money-lust, Duddy, but I'm afraid for you. You're two people, that's why. The scheming little bastard I saw so easily and the fine, intelligent boy underneath that your grandfather, bless him, saw. But you're coming of age soon and you'll have to choose. A boy can be two, three, four potential people, but a man is only one. He murders the others.*
> *There's a brute inside you, Duddel—a regular behemoth—and this being a hard world it would be the easiest thing for you to let it overpower you. Don't, Duddel, Be a gentleman. A <u>mensh</u>.* (328)

Sammy Glick was a "scheming little bastard" from beginning to end. He was made that way and he will end that way. Richler takes the Sammy model, opens it up and inserts a second prototype that is totally different from the first. Duddy is indeed two people, but as we find out when he appears in Richler's later novels, he never does choose between them. Although at the end of his apprenticeship he feels like a success, and as readers we hope that the "fine, intelligent boy" will eventually win out, Richler leaves all options open.

Richler's own Duddy-like streak of ruthlessness shows itself in the way he fictionally demolishes friends who have crossed him in some way. Richler even goes Duddy one better by including family members in the general carnage. Richler's real life estrangement from his mother and brother are generally known. Indeed his implacable hostility toward the mother who left his father when Richler was thirteen provides an endless stream of literary invention. In *The Acrobats* the mother is merely ludicrously unfaithful; in *Son of a Smaller Hero* she cruelly taunts her husband, manipulates and lies to her son, and is finished off with a massive heart attack. In *Duddy Kravitz* the mother is dead before the story begins. Later, in *St.*

Urbain's Horseman, she springs back to life as a stereotypical, guilt-mongering Jewish mother whose son cannot wait to have her out of his house. Eventually, in *Joshua Then and Now* she climbs to new heights, or new lows, as a stripper and porno star.

With *The Apprenticeship of Duddy Kravitz* Richler broke into the big leagues of prose fiction. He found his authentic voice and demonstrated his immense skill at literary parody. In his portrait of Duddy Kravitz, he also laid bare the energy, ruthlessness, sacrifice, and guilt that his own success and happiness required. This would be turned on its head in his next novel, *The Incomparable Atuk.*

The Incomparable Atuk: Making the Punishment Fit the Crime

> *My object all sublime*
> *I shall achieve in time—*
> *To let the punishment fit the crime—*
> *The punishment fit the crime;*
> *And make each prisoner pent*
> *Unwillingly represent*
> *A source of innocent merriment,*
> *Of innocent merriment.*

"Let the punishment fit the crime," sings the Mikado in Gilbert and Sullivan's operetta. Let there be "vengeance connected with writing," and let me "on the coarsest level, get even with the world for slights imaginary or real," proclaims Richler in his 1971 interview with David Godfrey. And in *The Incomparable Atuk* getting even is what Richler does!

Richler uses his fifth novel to mount an incredibly coarse attack on those who have slighted him, and on those who just happened to be around when his vengeance was let loose. Having achieved critical success with *The Apprenticeship of Duddy Kravitz* but still desperately short of cash, Richler turns the sweet taste of victory into a bitter battle against those who arbitrate literary taste, those who seek celebrity of any kind, and those who take themselves or their success more seriously than he thinks is reasonable. He also excoriates excess of any kind, even in the area of "doing good."

Although the savage wit of satire is supposed to have a corrective intent (the rationale being that people who see their faults writ large tend to improve their behavior), this concept has not actually been verified. In fact the opposite is more likely to occur. Those who might benefit from seeing their behavior mocked either don't recognize themselves at all, or if they do, are mortally offended. They are more likely to sue the satirist than change their own actions or beliefs. So it is that *The Incomparable Atuk*, set in Toronto and seemingly concerned mainly with Torontonians, was most enjoyed by readers who did not recognize themselves. Those who did see themselves in the novel were very angry.

Up until his fifth novel, Richler had used parody to create ironic undertones in otherwise semi-realistic, semi-biographical tales. In *The Acrobats* there were so many parodies that they threatened to swamp the plot. And in *Son of a Smaller Hero* and *The Apprenticeship of Duddy Kravitz*—his hotly denied but undeniably biographical books—he occasionally and memorably broke into the wild exaggeration of satire. Although the satire was routinely condemned as evidence of ethnic self-hatred by his Montreal Jewish critics, he decided to go for broke and write a full-blooded satire in *Atuk*.

In this novel, satire clearly rules. All human frailty is held up to merciless ridicule. And now that most of the original targets are gone and largely forgotten, it is easy to see that their culpability is not unique. In fact Richler gives some of his own worst traits to the central character: the "Eskimo" Atuk. Then he places his clear-sighted moral outrage in a second character—Jean Paul McEwan—who observes Atuk from above the fray: commenting, judging, and giving the novel an ethical center that we can trust.

Atuk—with his criminal past, hygienic challenges, mediocre poetry, and inexplicable appeal to women—functions as an example of what Richler considered the abysmal state of literary taste in Canada at the time. That he himself was now being praised by a literary establishment he disdained, caused Richler deep dismay. He therefore placed a straw man—an "Eskimo" poet whom he could with impunity knock down—in a family situation that parodied his own. He also burdened Atuk with his own money problems that literary success did not as yet cure.

To augment his income Atuk brings his family to Toronto, locks them in his basement, and puts them to work turning out poorly made "Eskimo" sculptures that he acknowledges are "junk." In this, Atuk's father, brothers and sisters parallel Richler's father, uncles and aunt who slave in the family scrap yard where they work with real junk. They may also suggest the family members that Richler keeps locked up in his brain to be used in parodies and satires that some of his critics have unkindly called "junk" in their reviews.

Atuk has so many faults that when he finally meets his maker by way of Twentyman's "dreadful equipment," it is his greed and not his cannibalism that does him in. But it is obvious that Richler intends the punishment to fit the real crime (murder) rather than the rigged television game that actually has Atuk put his head on the chopping block. In Gilbert and Sullivan's *Mikado,* the Lord High Executioner's chopping block has a double function: to punish the guilty and entertain the "innocent" multitudes. Twentyman's equipment—since it is the central object on stage during the TV quiz show, "Stick out your neck—is also obviously designed for entertainment. In *The Mikado* the Lord High Executioner cheerily chopped off heads with a "short, sharp shock/From a cheap and chippy chopper on a big black block." In *the Incomparable Atuk* a resounding "KER-PLUNCK" signals the end of Atuk. Indeed Twentyman's dreadful equipment begins and ends the book while serving first to introduce Atuk and then to take his life. It links Richler's novel with Gilbert and Sullivan's operetta at the same time as it links the amoral Atuk with the crime-busting Jean-Paul McEwan.

It takes courage for an author to put part of himself in a reprehensible little Eskimo fraud. It also takes courage to put himself in the person of a woman—even a woman journalist with strong moral convictions—who has already given herself a man's name because she feels that women journalists get no respect. Richler's drag persona stands on the author's moral platform and declares her judgments to the characters inside the book, and at the same time to Richler's readers in the world outside. This is important because crafting punishments to fit crimes goes on in both places at once. Jean-Paul McEwan—hard-hitting, high-principled newspaper journalist—ferrets out crime and corruption in high places and low, taking Atuk's measure long before anyone else does. Richler writes himself with ironic flourish into this reporter extraordinaire, and then doubles the irony by having Jean-Paul fall in love with someone who she thinks is a lovely girl. This "girl," fortunately, turns out to be Sergeant Jock Wilson of the Royal Canadian Mounted Police, temporarily in drag as part of an undercover hunt for communist subversives. Jean-Paul is cross-dressed herself in a scheme to ferret out corruption on the University of Toronto campus. She therefore spends most of the story disguised as a man, a role she obviously enjoys (as Sergeant Wilson finds he quite likes wearing silken undies).

This whole sub-plot is a parody on the Shakespearean convention where boys played women's parts. In certain romantic comedies the plot called for these women characters to disguise themselves as men; then at the end they would take off their disguise to reveal their true stage identity, which invariably signaled the happy ending. But all the time the audience was deliciously aware that the "women" taking off their male disguise were really boys playing the part. In Richler's satiric parody, although Jock Wilson and Jean-Paul McEwan take off their gender disguise, they cannot enjoy a romantic happy ending until Jock (still in drag) has competed in the Miss Universe contest. Whether Jock's cross-dressing will continue beyond the end of the novel only the author knows for sure. But it is suggested that the cross-dressing at the start may mean that the two will remain star-crossed lovers at the end.

Because Richler wants us to recognize Jean-Paul McEwan as his alter ego, he brings her into action right at the beginning of the story, viewing from a plane the unloading of crates containing Twentyman's dreadful equipment. She also inquires about the Eskimo Atuk, who will encounter the equipment in a most unfortunate way. Jean-Paul smokes a Schimmelpenninck—the cigar Richler was known to fancy at that time.

> Even Jean-Paul McEwan, the most astute journalist in Canada, couldn't find out what, if anything, was in which crate. She had to return to Toronto empty-handed.
> Worse. Her chartered aeroplane was ordered to circle the field until another one had landed safely.
> 'Who in the hell's in that other plane?' McEwan demanded, outraged.
> 'Some Eskimo. Wait.' The pilot listened in on his radio. 'His name's Atuk.'
> McEwan lit up another Schimmelpenninck as her plane was obliged to circle the field for another ten minutes. 'I'm going to remember that name,' she said. (1-2)

Between the Schimmelpenninck and the outrage, Jean-Paul's role as Richler's mouthpiece is subtly established. At the end, when Atuk is discovered to have eaten an American colonel who had disappeared in the Arctic wilds, Toronto newspapers—citing Atuk's moral deficiencies because of his Eskimo background—all come out against his being punished.

> 'While we would be the last to condone cannibalism,' the editorial writer on the <u>Standard</u> wrote, we do feel that Atuk, a simple man, is a special case. US Army officers had no business in his land, disturbing an age-old and time-honored way of life. Flatly, pardon him.'...(169)
> Only Jean-Paul McEwan...demanded the death sentence for Atuk.(171)

Since Richler's and Jean-Paul's views are the same, the greedy Atuk goes on what he is assured will be a quiz show rigged in his favour, called

"STICK OUT YOUR NECK." Atuk foolishly complies, and Twentyman's dreadful equipment does the rest.

While we laugh and shudder at Atuk's shoddy behavior as he travels through the novel, we are always aware of Jean-Paul McEwan's moral judgment as a counter weight. We also notice that Atuk's story is not the only one in the novel that bears his name, because Richler's satire proceeds along several story tracks all at the same time. One track is particularly interesting for those who know of the feud between Richler and Toronto literary and theatre critic, Nathan Cohen. In the novel, he is called "Seymour Bone," and in the Richler papers at the University of Calgary Library, Special Collections/Archives we find the reason that Richler decides to skewer him.

The relationship between Richler and Nathan Cohen appears to be very friendly in letters written between 1954 and 1955, where each of Nathan Cohen's letters ends with "All my love to you and Cathy"(Richler's first wife). In 1955 as well, Cohen—as script editor in the drama department of CBC-TV—writes Richler a long letter regarding his second novel *Son of a Smaller Hero*. In the letter he states that Richler "had created the Jewish community scene graphically, and created some moving, deeply felt characters." Furthermore he found that "one of the very best things in the book [was] the excellent revelation of the void which Melech's family [had] moved into." Near the end of the letter Cohen states, "Let me make this clear, Mordecai, we all of us thought it so good that we were eager to match opinions, and discuss it." At the very end he writes, "As for the Montreal Jews, if they don't like it, to hell with them! They should be proud that a writer of your talent and capacity came out of that environment." In 1956, Cohen conducts an empathetic interview with Richler in England, published as "A conversation with Mordecai Richler."

Then in 1957—after the publication of Richler's third novel, *A Choice of Enemies*—Nathan Cohen (still professing himself a good friend) writes a devastating essay in the *Tamarack Review*: an essay called "Heroes of the

Richler View." Here he reverses his earlier praise for Richler's characters, and writes:

> *Most of the men and women who pass through his pages are, by design, empty, trivial, disgusting, happy to vegetate in the safe cage of traditional principles, alarmed beyond belief by the perilous freedom of truth-seeking. They are so small, so worthless, so...undeserving of compassion, that they are not worth caring about.* (*Tamarack Review*, 53)

Having demolished the peripheral characters, Cohen assaults Richler's "heroes"—the main characters who reflect Richler's deepest values even while being humanly flawed.

> *Here is the cruelest irony: the charges the heroes of the Richler view make against their antagonists apply, with equal validity, to themselves. They are selfish, oblivious to human dignity, cold, insensitive, conscienceless, wantonly destructive of personal relations. They have no nobility of spirit. Indeed they are worse than the people around them since they presume to know better and insist on their superiority.* (*Tamarack Review*, 56-7)

Finally, with one swipe Cohen erases all the kind things he has previously said about his friend's writing.

> *With three novels to his credit, it is no longer feasible to think of Mordecai Richler as a beginning writer, or to cushion criticism of his work by reason of his youth. It was possible to do so with* <u>The Acrobats</u> *and* <u>Son of a Smaller Hero</u>, *since they were so inherently autobiographical. Under the circumstances the slovenly, undisciplined craftsmanship, the unsettling ambivalence of thought, the contrived violence and abundant bedwetting were understandable, if not pardonable.* (*Tamarack Review*, 57)

What was obviously unpardonable for Richler was that a friend who had privately praised his work would suddenly shaft him so cruelly in public. With publication of *The Incomparable Atuk,* Richler shafts Nathan Cohen right back.

The character that resembles Nathan Cohen, named "Seymour Bone" (a name that already has "potty humor" undertones), is described as coming out of the West "On flat broad feet in 1944,...Out of the West to conquer Toronto: the cruel capital. A fat ungainly redheaded boy,...He fitted in nowhere. The intellectuals put him down for a backward, if amusing bumpkin, and the others found him a bore" (*Atuk,* 59). Seymour Bone's eating habits are disgusting, and his reputation as a stern theatre critic results from his having left his first assignment well before the play ended because of embarrassing digestive problems.

> *Bone went to the theatre constipated and woke up a national figure. But his newly-won reputation was able to ruin his pleasure for years to come. For the truth was that Bone was delighted by most plays, specially if they were full of salty jokes or good-looking girls, but he felt that if he didn't walk out on every second one people would say he was going soft....But as Bone's celebrity increased, even as his insults grew more shrill, he became personally unpopular. Nobody asked him to parties any more.* (*Tamarack Review,* 63)

Having—by proxy—impugned Nathan Cohen's intellect and reputation as a critic (a reputation that Cohen particularly cherished), and having demolished his social life, Richler gives the proxy knife a final twist. Seymour Bone's wife, Ruthie, reveals to her husband that she is pregnant, warning him at the same time that their baby might have a "sort of chocolate-y" color. This triggers an immediate recollection of an earlier episode in the book where Joseph, the tall, good-looking black man who washes windows for the wives of the cultural elite, was found with Ruthie in a compromising situation. Seymour Bone is understandably aghast at the thought of explaining a chocolate colored baby to his friends and Richler has added cuckolding to his revenge.

Humiliating a thinly disguised Nathan Cohen in his novel as Cohen had six years earlier maligned him in an essay is Richler's neat trick in making the punishment fit the crime. At the same time, the portrait is so mortifying that Cohen could not take the chance of suing Richler for defamation, since too many people were already chuckling at what Richler had done.

Richler again protects himself from a possible lawsuit when he creates a sexually enhanced version of the swimmer Marilyn Bell—"Canada's Darling"—in his book's portrait of Bette Dolan. He deliberately places his fictional character in the company of real life celebrities such as "Deanna Durbin, Marilyn Bell, Barbara Ann Scott, and Joyce Davidson." By stating that his eighteen-year-old marathon swimmer, Bette Dolan, was "the first woman to swim Lake Ontario in less than twenty hours," Richler contrasts her accomplishment with Marilyn Bell's, who at the age of sixteen became the first person to ever swim Lake Ontario. Richler thus draws attention to what he is doing while avoiding a law suit. He can now go on to describe his version of "Canada's Darling" in any way he sees fit. And what he does is take the known facts surrounding the swim: that Marilyn beat the 34 year old American professional swimmer, Florence Chadwick (who had been offered $10,000 to swim across Lake Ontario, but gave up after twenty hours), and the Toronto swimming star, Winnie Roach Leuszler (who also quit the race before the end). He includes the well-publicized facts that Marilyn Bell had declared she was taking on the challenge "to uphold the honor of Canada"; that her coach who was traveling in a boat beside her kept moving the boat forward to make her swim up to it; and that Marilyn felt she had a tremendous responsibility to set a good example because Canadians had taken her to their hearts.

In Richler's version it is Bette's father who is her coach and who spurs her on when she thinks she can go no further.

> *But Bette had already been in the lake for sixteen hours. The plucky girl had come thirty-four miles. Thrashing about groggily, her eyes glazed, she began to weep. 'can't feel my legs any more…can't…think…going to drown…'*
> *'All right,' Dolan said, gesturing his girl towards the launch, 'we'll pull you in now, kid.'*
> *But as Bette, making an enormous effort, swam within inches of the launch Gord Dolan pulled ahead a few more yards.*
> *'Come on, honey. Come to Daddy.'*
> *Again she started for the launch and again Gord Dolan pulled away.*
> *'You see,' he shouted at her. 'You can do it.' (Atuk, 15)*

The reaction of the crowd when the exhausted teenager stumbles on shore compares in frenzy with the crowd's reaction to Marilyn Bell's historic achievement. The fictional Bette, like the real life Marilyn, becomes a national heroine. However, it is not the swimming that Richler satirizes (other than the father's duplicity in forcing the girl to go on beyond the point of danger). It is rather Marilyn Bell's belief that she belongs to all of Canada and must therefore set the highest standard by living an exemplary life. Richler satirizes this belief into Bette Dolan's decision to withhold herself sexually from any individual man, since she belongs to all the people of Canada.

Bette's high moral ground is undermined by the sneaky Atuk, who appeals to her sympathy by pretending he is impotent and "needs help." Bette, delighted to find that "helping" can be so much fun, encourages Atuk to "hit the bull's eye" long after Atuk has lost interest in the game. In fact, while Bette is belatedly discovering the joys of sex, Atuk is discovering Goldie Panofsky, a fat, smelly woman who is more his type. After losing Atuk's attention, Bette finds other men to "help"—a situation that Jean-Paul McEwan deplores in her newspaper column:

> *The beautiful girl, having fallen—so to speak—once, is now falling for others as well. She thinks she is helping these men!*
> *The girl is no longer pretty and her language has become…salty.*

> *This is one of the saddest tales even this world-hardened reporter has ever had to write because, like Canadians everywhere, I believed in the girl. I loved her. (146)*

In Bette Dolan, Richler satirizes women who consider themselves to be "God's gift to men." At the same time he is having fun with God's words in the Bible where God says: "It is not good that the man should be alone; I will make him a help meet for him." In Genesis 2:18 the word "meet" means "fitting," But Bette takes it more in the sense of "help-mate." She first protects her purity because she cannot be false to Canada by giving herself to any one man. Then, after discovering that the "funny stuff" is rather nice, Bette becomes the all-Canadian helpmate—"Canada's Darling" in a sense unforeseen by those who first called her that.

Why Richler takes on Marilyn Bell may be simply that he feels swimming Lake Ontario is not such a big deal, and that the public's priorities are skewed. Or he may simply have looked for a recognizable public figure to use in his all out war on celebrities. Whatever Richler's motive, he punishes Bette Dolan for first believing her own publicity and considering herself too good for any man, and later for pretending to be performing acts of charity when she is actually just having sex. Her discovery that the "funny stuff" is really fun changes her from a lady to a tramp.

Bette's male counterpart in the world of sexually available athletic celebrities is Jersey Joe Marchette—billed by his trainer as "THE WORLD'S BEST DEVELOPED...BLIND...NEGRO!" He also moonlights as Joseph—the tall handsome black man who cleans windows for Toronto's elite, and is lusted after by the ladies he works for. In this situation he is certainly not blind, nor is he degraded by "helping" the many customers who demand his services: unless being subservient to white folk, and having to "perform" at the ladies' commands is already degradation enough. Richler is of course satirizing the supposedly inexhaustible energy of black men. The ladies, in turn, are punished for taking the term "handyman" too literally when each one finds out that "her Joe" is not as exclusively hers as she had imagined.

All characters in *The Incomparable Atuk* are in some way connected. Joseph, popping up at one lady's house after another, is one of the connecting links and various members of the Panofsky family link up the rest. Through Goldie Panofsky who becomes Atuk's blushing bride to be, the Panofskys connect to the book's main character. At the same time they caricature certain attitudes that Richler finds abhorrent. Mr. Panofsky beats up Christians and conducts an insane experiment designed to prove that all Christians look alike. He does this by exchanging identity bracelets on infants at the maternity hospital. When he is arrested and the police ask him to help untangle the terrible mess he has made in people's lives, his answer is hauntingly reminiscent of words spoken by Nazi concentration camp doctors on trial after the Second World War: "I'd like to help you, captain. But there were so many, so many names. It was all in the interest of scientific research, you know"(*Atuk*, 130). Panofsky's punishment, as well as being sent to jail, is to be associated—by his words and beliefs—with Nazi criminal behavior.

Panofsky, who in his daily life hides rabid anti-Christian feelings under his cloak of gentle Jew, has a second son who calls himself Rory Peel. An assimilated Jew, Rory carries out bomb shelter drills with his family during which the children routinely kick, punch, and otherwise brutalize their German family maid. Rory's punishment at the end is to be locked in his bomb shelter by Brunhilde, the maid, who drives away in the family car.

Rory—an advertising executive—was also the one who brought Atuk out of the frozen north, promoting his "Eskimo poetry" to the Toronto literati. In this track of the story, and in all the sections that deal with Atuk's clunky poems and his family's production of junky sculpture, Richler derides the western world's fascination with all things Inuit: suggesting that most arbiters of taste cannot tell good art from junk.

Atuk, as a young hustler trying to make a buck, is closely related to the young Duddy Kravitz without Duddy's redeeming "David" side. At one point in the story, Atuk says of himself that he is "a somebody" now: a deliberate echo of Duddy's flawed achievement. When the Eskimo Atuk falls in love with the Jewish Goldie Panofsky, both fathers—the Old One and the old Panofsky—give the lovers ethnic warnings.

> "I do not wish to hear of marriage with a non-Eskimo girl."
> "You know something, Old One. You're a bigot. You've never overcome your igloo mentality."
> "I'm proud of my heritage."
> "So am I. Only I refuse to be imprisoned by it."
> "Tell me, Atuk. What would you do about the children?..."
> "How would it be for me to sit your little half-breed on my lap and he wouldn't be able to speak an Eskimo word?..."
> "Shall I go to their home. To be stared at. An Eskimo. Would I feel relaxed there, Atuk. I'd have to wash and eat with cutlery...."
> "So you'd make a few adjustments. A big deal...."
> "We are the chosen pagans, my son. We have a message for the world." (83-86)

Since Richler had married his own Christian love, Florence, only three years before publishing *Atuk*, parental arguments against intermarriage would still be fresh in his mind, and he obviously does not fault Atuk for wanting to marry Goldie. However, Richler does have a message for the world, and Atuk's final punishment is related to that message. In *The Apprenticeship of Duddy Kravitz*, Duddy's uncle said that Duddy had two sides: a fine, intelligent boy and a ruthless money-grubbing pusher. Atuk represents the dark side of Duddy—the pushy, money-grubbing, ruthlessly self-centered part that must be destroyed if he wants to become a decent human being. After Atuk undergoes the guillotine's KER-PLUNK, Richler never again creates a destructively double-sided main character; nor does he create a protagonist as ethically challenged as Atuk. In the novels that follow this one, the central characters will be decent men with only the common weaknesses of mankind. They may not be great heroes, but they do the best they can.

Richler's message to mankind is the same as Gilbert and Sullivan's in *The Mikado:* one way or another, crimes will be punished—if not in life, then in literature. In *The Incomparable Atuk* Richler savages the things that trouble him most, starting with the way Canadian writers, himself included, become celebrities. How can a writer take his success seriously, or genuinely enjoy being lionized, when he believes that a city like Toronto will applaud any artist who arrives with sufficient hype? Atuk is genuinely incomparable among Richler's heroes in that he has no talent and is utterly irredeemable. Yet in this book Richler has a rattling good time settling scores left and right. His next novel, *Cocksure,* in spite of many hilarious moments, is more painful to read.

Cocksure: An Honest Man in a Nightmare World

Irony: saying one thing and meaning the opposite.

Parody: acknowledged borrowing of a literary work or convention to imply critical distance.

Satire: savage mockery of human vices and frailties with an eye to mankind's improvement.

Dystopia: the opposite of utopia. A fully realized imaginary place, all aspects of which are appalling.

Described by Richler as a *jeu d'esprit,* a light-hearted fantasy that helped unblock his creative juices during the writing of *St. Urbain's Horseman, Cocksure* is both darker and deeper than its author cared to claim. Published eleven years after *A Choice of Enemies, Cocksure* mocks the illusion of choice and the hope of happiness to which an ordinary man clings. Part satire, part parody, part dystopia in the spirit of Orwell's *1984* and Huxley's *Brave New World, Cocksure* tells the story of a good man trying to function in a world gone startlingly wrong.

The setting is London, England in the 1960s. The central character, Mortimer Griffin, works as an editor at Oriole Press—a publishing company recently absorbed into a multinational conglomerate headed by the sinister Star Maker—a man of many parts, few of them originally his own. Star Maker's contribution to the film industry is the manufacture of synthetic movie stars, none of them distinguishable from the real thing. His contribution to science is to hire only the healthiest people as employees—their ultimate purpose being to supply him with transplants of body parts as his own wear out or get diseased.

His greatest accomplishment in this field is to follow up on a disgruntled employee's profanity: "go fuck yourself." Star Maker immediately expropriates the reproductive system of a recently hired secretary—and does! He is now happily pregnant, eagerly awaiting the birth of his heir. This reproductive strategy goes even beyond the implication of his personal company logo, two snakes coupled: an ancient Greek symbol of Zeus having sex with his mother Rhea, both in the form of snakes. Star Maker's love affair with himself only takes this incestuous situation one step further. And Richler pushes the acceptable medical technique of transplanting organs to grotesque extremes.

Well before Star Maker became the first man to impregnate himself, he became the first film mogul to create non-living movie stars who could be deflated like balloons when they were no longer needed, and packed away in boxes until the next time. Unfortunately, these man-made actors developed needs and wishes like their human counterparts, refusing to be put away at the end of a film. They wore out and blew up, causing no end of fuss.

> "Which brings me to our triumph, Goy Boy III, the Mini-Goy. What a piece of work! Three expressions, Mortimer. Three. Walked very very nice. Talked in sentences as long as twelve words each…Mortimer, among actors Mini-goy passed for an intellectual. Women were crazy for him…We broke open the champagne and we called him, well, you know," the Star Maker said, whispering the celebrated Star's name once more. (140-41)
> In the middle of a picture, his fiftieth maybe, bang! zam! kazoom! He blew up. Disintegrated. Grips were wiping wet pieces of the Star off their faces. Grown men cried like babies. It was terrible, ghastly."
> (141)

Cocksure: An Honest Man in a Nightmare World

We are impressed by the reason this monstrously self-serving creature is called "Star Maker," and equally astounded by Richler's imaginative extension of a common term for film moguls. However, Star Maker's reference to his man-made stars as "Goy-Boys" points in a less amusing direction. "Goy" is the slur-term a Jew will use when he wants to elevate himself intellectually above Christians. The implication is that Christians might be more attractive but Jews are smarter. Star Maker's "stars" are designed to be boyishly handsome, attractively muscular, and engagingly stupid. While on one level this satirizes the public's worship of empty-headed pretty-boys in the film world, on a deeper level it ties in with the badgering suffered by Mortimer Griffin, the Gentile (and gentle) hero of Richler's dangerously cockeyed world.

In a book deliberately called *Cocksure,* Mortimer definitely is not! But his persecutors, all of them Jews, are as cocky as they come. And this is the second time that Richler has written a novel in which a gentle WASP is stung to death by a pack of ferocious Jews. Star Maker—the patched monstrosity of mismatched bits and pieces, all taken from his now limbless, eyeless, or dead employees—has an engaging manner that belies the ruthless way he operates. But Shalinsky—the elderly Jew who hounds Mortimer about his religious affiliation—is unpleasant through and through. Similarly Ziggy Spicehandler—who replaces Mortimer in his home, his bed, and the affection of his wife and son—is presented as a thoroughly repellent human being. But, disgusting as Ziggy may be and obnoxious as Shalinsky certainly is, Star Maker will be the one to decree that Mortimer must die. To this menacing gang of three, Richler adds Hy Rosen—a bantam cock-of-the-walk who used to be Mortimer's good friend and co-editor at Oriole Press—that is until Mortimer confides the problems he is having with Shalinsky. After that Hy abruptly withdraws his friendship, leaving Mortimer to struggle alone.

Shalinsky's badgering attempts to shame Mortimer—who is and always was Christian—into admitting that he is actually a Jew, and a self-hating Jew at that, recall the unrelenting techniques of George Orwell's *Nineteen*

Eight-Four. In Orwell's dystopia, brutal forces combine to convince the hapless Winston Smith that he must renounce his human individuality, and become a mindless zombie like all the others who worship Big Brother. In the dangerously upside-down world of *Cocksure,* Mortimer—an earnest, upright, Canadian WASP living and working in "Swinging London"—hasn't a chance. His downfall begins when the elderly Shalinsky, a mature student in Mortimer's night-school class, insists that Mortimer must be Jewish because he is too well read to be Christian. When Mortimer protests, Shalinsky adds "self-hating Jew" to the label, and turns nasty. He asserts that while Mortimer is too intelligent to be anything but Jewish, he is too cowardly to own up to what he really is. Mortimer, stung by this racist compliment, is never more Waspish than when he refuses to join Shalinsky's select little Jewish intellectual club: and he pays dearly for his refusal.

This strand of the novel—taken for the most part from Richler's short story "Mortimer Griffin, Shalinsky, and how they solved the Jewish Problem"—is woven into the larger dangers of Star Maker's world. Whereas one man (Shalinsky) wants Mortimer's soul, the other (Star Maker) is only interested in Mortimer's body: specifically his so-called "marvy lymph system." Richler's original short story had an ironic "happy ending" in that Mortimer converted to Judaism, married Shalinsky's daughter, and decided to write for Shalinsky's Jewish newspaper. But *Cocksure* presents a darker vision: the book ends with Mortimer's futile attempts to outrun Star Maker's German execution squad—becoming a Jew by his fate, though not by birth.

In his earlier novel, *A Choice of Enemies,* Richler had written about an upright, uptight WASP living and working in the film and literary world of London. But this film world, although it turned against Norman Price, was not turned upside down; nor was Richler at that time writing a satire. Norman Price's Jewish friends became his enemies when he thrust a young, former Nazi in their midst; but they were already resentful of Norman because his impeccable behavior had made them feel uncomfortable.

Perhaps the book also made critics and readers feel uncomfortable, which would account for its cool reception. *Cocksure* on the other hand, being dirty, funny, and satirical, was highly praised.

Mortimer Griffin's story in *Cocksure*—in keeping with the definition of parody as imitation with ironic difference—becomes a satiric parody of *A Choice of Enemies*. The satire is directed against the "using and abusing" of "underlings" in the film and publishing business; the parody is a reworking in darker colors of Norman Price's fictional life. Both *A Choice of Enemies* and *Cocksure* tell a story of good but not perfect men struggling against an implacable fate. Norman Price and Mortimer Griffin are both Gentiles who are persecuted by Jews: Norman because he does not realize the danger of bringing a former Nazi into his circle of Jewish friends, and also because he disdains certain Jewish characteristics. Mortimer's persecution begins when he rears back too sharply at being considered Jewish—on the premise that Jews are smarter than Christians. While Norman ends up with a sadly diminished existence, Mortimer will end up dead. He, in effect, becomes one of Star Maker's "Goy-Boys": handsome, muscular, not too bright, but useful for Star Maker's purposes. After giving up his lymph system he will be packed away in a box. But unlike the virtual stars, Mortimer will be in that box forever. Star Maker, Greek-born but now mostly Jewish, thanks to the many "spare parts" he has taken from Jewish employees, will go on forever. But gentle Mortimer Griffin is completely expendable.

After five novels that contain less than perfect parents, Mordecai Richler has finally created the ultimate parental monstrosity. "You are my son," says Star Maker to one of his trusted underlings before depriving him of yet another body part. In Richler's dystopia, the doomed "children" of Star Maker live on in their "parent" rather than the other way around where parents see themselves as living on in the children to whom they give life. Moreover, just as people with Type O blood are considered to be "universal donors" because their blood is compatible with almost everyone else's, so Star Maker becomes a "universal recipient" because his employees supply him with every body part he needs.

Although Norman Price (in *A Choice of Enemies*) made some mistakes when he chose his friends, the affection of *Cocksure*'s Mortimer Griffin for the disgusting, degenerate Ziggy Spicehandler goes way beyond the meaning of bad choice. Again, because this is a satire and satire thrives on exaggeration, Ziggy is not only appalling in his hygiene and in his sexual behavior, but he also produces a cruelly mocking film about Mortimer that insults every value his friend holds dear. Because Mortimer is himself an honorable man he cannot understand the depth of Ziggy's depravity, or the extent of his cruelty under the banner of art. After moving into Mortimer's house and seducing his wife, Ziggy "demonstrates" in a chillingly perverse home movie that Mortimer's everyday decency is actually a laughable perversion. By stretching the meaning of "unsuitable friend" to encompass Ziggy, Richler practically exonerates Norman for his poor choice. Unfortunately, *Cocksure* is not usually seen as a parody of *A Choice of Enemies*, so a good deal of Richler's parodic intent is lost.

As he adds to his list of novels, Richler revisits the ones he wrote earlier, increasing the ferocity of his attack and choosing different targets. In *A Choice of Enemies*, it is Norman's timid approach to love and his inability to understand Jewish sensitivities that rouses Richler's ire, so that he has to bring him down. In *Cocksure,* it is the militantly self-righteous Jewish watchdogs—especially those who write for Jewish newspapers that call Richler himself a "self-hating Jew"—that he targets. Shalinsky is a dangerous and thoroughly despicable human being, as is Ziggy Spicehandler who seems to represent the utmost in disgusting behavior that Richler feels he can get away with. Mortimer Griffin, the nominal hero, is merely a hapless victim in *Cocksure*: a dystopia where the bad guys hold all the cards.

Parody involves an author's reassessment of someone else's literary work by playing it in another key. Richler carries this concept one step further by including his own earlier novels in the parody process. In *The Incomparable Atuk*, he revisits and revises certain beliefs about success that first appeared in *The Apprenticeship of Duddy Kravitz*. Then, when he comes to write *Cocksure*, it is the assumed complicity of an upright man in his own destruction about which Richler changes his mind.

Having lost his reputation, his home, and most of his friends, now running for his life, Mortimer Griffin is consoled by two very different women—the achingly lovely Polly Morgan who lives life as if it were a film script, and the solidly pragmatic teacher, Miss Ryerson. While young Polly soothes his fears of impotence by "jump-cutting" from seductive foreplay to relaxed pillow talk with no need for action in between, the elderly Miss Ryerson's unexpected sexual skills contribute to her good results as a teacher of young men. She thrives in the topsy-turvy world of *Cocksure*, where nothing is as it seems, by being infinitely adaptable and supremely confident—as Mortimer unfortunately is not.

> "God damn it, Miss Ryerson, you can't go around blowing school kids. It isn't done."
> "Don't you dare," Miss Ryerson said evenly, "take the Lord's name in vain in my presence."
> "Sorry."
> "Are you dead set against blowing, Mortimer?"
> "I wouldn't know how to answer that, Miss Ryerson. We've never discussed, well…sex."
> "<u>Put out that cigarette immediately</u>."
> "Yes."
> "You ask me if you may smoke, I courteously acquiesce. Then you take the Lord's name in vain. And now you wish to discuss sex with me."
> "Sorry."(172)

Turning from Miss Ryerson's cockeyed values to Polly's seemingly safe arms, Mortimer—now being followed by Star Maker's execution squad—asks Polly for help. He tells her to run to a public telephone to phone the police.

> *Polly ran. She ran and ran. The first telephone booth she came to was empty, which wouldn't have done at all. She continued, breathless, to the next booth where, fortunately, a long-haired teen-ager was chattering endlessly, unaware that a man's life was at stake. Rat-tat-tat, Polly went, banging her sixpence against the glass. Rat-tat-tat. The teen-ager was done, just in time, Polly sensed, and she entered the booth. Polly deposited her sixpence and dialed nine nine nine. "Metropolitan Police here. Yes?"*
> *Polly smiled warmly. "Hello! Hello! Is there anyone there?" the officer asked. Gratefully, Polly hung up, hung up without speaking, and on the wide screen that was her mind's eye, sirens sounded, police cars heaving into Beaufort Street in the nick of time. (215-16)*

Polly's wide-screen world is superficially attractive, and pleasantly familiar from our own movie-going experience. We therefore consider Polly less dangerous than Star Maker who feeds on his employees even while he calls them his "children." But Polly is just as crazy in her way as Star Maker is in his. And for Mortimer, whose real world has fallen apart, Polly is the last temptation. Although at first she seems to provide just the respite from trouble that Mortimer needs, when action is called for, she seals his fate.

As Richler mocked literary celebrity (among other things) in *The Incomparable Atuk*, so he now attacks the film and publishing worlds on which (at the time of writing *Cocksure*) his livelihood depends. Although the setting is nominally London, we are actually in a fantastic, unreal place where almost everything that happens is grotesque and cruel. But since it is Richler's fantasy, his dystopia is funny and awful at the same time. Shalinsky, who trumpets through his newspaper that the so-called Christian Mortimer Griffin is actually a Jew in denial, combines in one small, stoop-shouldered, cigarette-ash-strewn old man the implacable self-righteousness of Richler's paternal grandfather—dramatized as Melech in *Son of a Smaller Hero*—and the blood-hound call to judgment of the entire Montreal Jewish Press. By making Shalinsky so relentless in his hounding of Mortimer, so sure that he is right while actually being wrong, Richler shows up the wrong-headed self-righteousness of his own tormentors. Shalinsky hinges his implacable belief that Mortimer is a Jew on the Yiddish phrase *ein yiddishe kop*, which means "a Jewish head," and signifies (to Jews) that the person is smart. By maniacally trying to destroy a Gentile who refuses to identify intelligence with being Jewish, Shalinsky does to Mortimer's psyche what the Star Maker, by laying claim to Mortimer's lymph system, will do to his life.

While he satirizes people he considers dangerous and deplorable, Richler also mocks himself. In this book it is in the person of Mortimer's Jewish friend and colleague, Hy Rosen, who immediately turns against the hapless Mortimer when he hears about Shalinsky's allegations. A short, quick-tempered pugnacious fellow with a tall, beautiful, adoring Christian wife, who protects him from getting hurt when he struts the London streets at night looking for Nazis to beat up, Hy's home life is everything that Mortimer's is not. The Rosens have a joyously acrobatic sex life, with only enough pretence on Diana Rosen's part to keep her husband feeling like the conquering hero he thinks himself to be. The lovely, understanding Diana serves as the grateful valentine Richler sends his wife Florence in every novel from this one on. The laughably yet dangerously aggressive Hy, who cuts off friends for slight real or imagined, stands for Richler with the chip on his shoulder writ large.

While he satirizes Jews who make war on unoffending Christians; women who live in the la la land of Hollywood movies; progressive schools where children run wild and grading for marks is considered an unacceptable infringement on their rights; and corporate moguls who use, abuse, and then discard what is left of their employees; Richler considers the hapless plight of the ordinary decent man living in a world he does not understand and in which he does not belong.

When Richler wrote *A Choice of Enemies*, the book was not particularly well received. When he wrote on a similar theme in *Cocksure*, he won the Canadian Governor General's Award. The difference between the two books is that in *A Choice of Enemies*, Richler (except for some clever parody) is essentially serious. When he came to write *Cocksure*, he had already mastered parody in *The Apprenticeship of Duddy Kravitz* and satire in *The Incomparable Atuk*. He therefore came up with an outrageous parody/satire/dystopia crammed full of cruel and dirty jokes, and the critics were enchanted. In the novels that followed *Cocksure*, Richler would take on serious themes in a serious way, while weaving in the comedy, parody, and satire that would give his best novels their distinctive edge.

St. Urbain's Horseman: Shoveling Trouble in the Stables of the Lord

"Tell you what's going over biggest today," Stein said. "Location novels. A novel constructed round one expensive set, taking you behind the scenes, where glamorous and eccentric characters meet…something with gritty realism….If you take the kitchen sink one step further, where are you?…the public toilet." (Richler's working notes to *Cocksure* in the University of Calgary Library Archives))

Unburdening himself now, Jake released the sewer gates. (Horseman, 180)

In *St Urbain's Horseman,* Richler's profoundly serious yet extremely funny novel, he takes up an idea he had for *Cocksure* but never got around to using. The idea was that the lowly toilet in its many forms could serve both comedy and tragedy, at times acting as a bridge between the two. While critics have lamented the many seemingly random references to lavatories, sewers, bad smells, filthy habits, and various sizes and shapes of excrement in the book, there is indeed method to Richler's scatological madness. For the most part he uses lavatory symbolism to connect characters, plot elements and themes in an intricate subterranean sewage system. For the rest, he amuses himself and his readers with "potty humor" related to his main character's problems in "letting go."

In keeping with the idea of making "the public toilet" a central location, Richler gives Jake Hersh, his central character, a latrine-related name. As Canadians refer to their toilet as "the John," so in England it is known as "the Jake" or "Jakes." But since Richler likes to squeeze at least two meanings out of a name if he can, Jake's full name—Jacob—comes from the Bible where Jacob is the son of Isaac and the third Patriarch of Israel. While the Jake part of his name involves him with a slimy little accountant named Harry Stein (whom Jake refers to as a "twisted little fart," and "lump of shit"), the Jacob part of his name leads him into a parody of Jacob's stealing a blessing from his dying father Isaac.

Since Richler's father, Moses Isaac Richler, died while this novel was being written, the stolen-blessing scene has real life resonance. The biblical Jacob had used deceit by impersonating the hairiness of his older brother Esau when he went to ask his blind old father to give him the first born son's blessing. Jacob Hersh uses deceit when he visits his dying father who, entranced by the comic antics of Jackie Gleeson on television, does not look at his son. To attract his father's attention, Jacob Hersh pretends to be a close friend of Jackie Gleeson's; and his father reacts with pleasure and respect. As Richler's parodies go, this is a very simple one, but it captures the bewildered love of a son who wants his father's blessing and cannot get it without deceit. For one brief moment, Jacob Hersh and Mordecai Richler are fused with the biblical Jacob who tricks his father into giving him a blessing that would otherwise have been withheld.

On the Jake side of the story, toilet symbolism may well have suggested itself to Richler when he turned aside from writing *Horseman* to dash off the satirical *Cocksure,* which functioned as a literary purgative. But once he returned to writing his serious book, the symbolism took on a life of its own, permeating both the lighter and the weightier parts of the novel. Nowhere is this fusion of comic and tragic elements brought together more dramatically than in the sequence where Herky, Jake's brother-in-law, comes to visit and insists on making a tour of London's lavatories.

> *But Herky Soloway was a special case. In London, above all, he wished to pay obeisances at the shrine of the incomparable Thomas Crapper, repository of stools immortal, where the Cascade had first*

St. Urbain's Horseman: Shoveling Trouble in the Stables of the Lord 89

> *been successfully flushed and the Niagara invented. Herky, warming to his subject, told Jake of the sparkling enamel toilets of Copenhagen, each bowl a joy to behold....* (232)
> *"Watch this." With a flick of the wrist, Herky flushed the toilet. "It's going on everywhere, day and night. Now you take the Fraser River for instance. More than once a day the untreated contents of one hundred thousand toilet bowls empty into it."*
> *[To which Jake murmurs] "That's a lot of shit, Herky."* (392)

The conjunction of "Fraser River" into which "one hundred thousand toilet bowls empty," and a man called, "Herky," (which sounds suspiciously like a diminutive of Hercules) sends out alarm bells. And what the bells suggest is that this is a joking reference to the fifth labor of Hercules, strongest and most famous of Greek mythical heroes, who diverted two rivers to run through the Augean stables flushing out manure excreted by thirty thousand oxen for thirty years. "A lot of shit," indeed. And a popular English translation of the Hercules myth is to be found in the writings of James G. Frazer. By tossing off this rhapsodic reference to the labors of Hercules, Richler signals that Herky's obsession with toilets may have a larger significance than simple comic relief. And a somber example of water flushing away excrement is not hard to find:

> *The women often lapped up their food like dogs; the only source of water was right next to the latrine, and this thin stream also served to wash away the excrement. There the women stood and drank or tried to take a little water with them in some container while next to them their fellow sufferers sat on the latrines. And throughout it all the female guards hit them with clubs. And while this was going on the S.S. walked up and down and watched.* (175 and 271)
> *"Mengele cannot have been there all the time."*
> *"In my opinion, always, Night and Day."* (272)

With Herky's "day and night" reversed as "Night and Day," Richler draws a graphic picture of female inmates in the Nazi death camps, humiliated by having to defecate in open latrines under the watchful eyes of brutal guards, and suffering the omnipresent scrutiny of the sadistic Mengele who was liable at any moment to choose one of them for the mutilating experiments he called "scientific."

To combat the horrors perpetrated in Nazi death camps under the watchful eyes of Doktor Josef Mengele, seemingly allowed by an indifferent God who does not intervene, Jake creates a Jewish superhero: the righteous Horseman of St. Urbain Street. He will avenge in fiction what Jake (and Richler) could not avenge in fact, and will become—for the author and his character—the Jewish equivalent of the mythic hero Hercules.

That the Horseman doesn't actually exist is a problem for Jake Hersh, but not an insurmountable one. If pictures in the mind such as the sickening treatment of Jews in Nazi camps can make us despair, then visual fantasies of the Horseman riding his white stallion "over the olive-green fields of upper Galilee" can raise our spirits. And this is one of the functions the Horseman performs for Jake: he provides an alternative set of pictures for the mind's eye, and thereby offers consolation to the heart. At a time when Jake is struggling with feelings of unworthiness, doubt and guilt; when upheavals in the household because of his difficult, visiting mother have tried his last shreds of patience and Harry Stein's perverted escapades are leading Jake, along with Harry, ever closer to jail; when life's possibilities seem to be closing in and shutting down: the Horseman, strong, valiant, and free of life's petty encumbrances, represents everything that Jake himself is not, but wishes that he could be. Although the Horseman's central role is to track down enemies of the Jews and mete out punishment, his importance to Jake is greater than that. Fashioned out of bits and pieces of Christian, Jewish, and Greco/Roman mythology, the Horseman's main task at the moment is to track down Doktor Josef Mendele and exact vengeance.

> The *Doktor* was reputed to keep armed bodyguards, maybe four of them. Certainly he kept a weapon handy himself. Say a service revolver tucked under his pillow or an automatic rifle leaning

> *against the wall of his villa with the barred windows off an unmarked road in the jungle, between Puerto San Vincente and the border fortress of Carlos Antonio Lopes, on the Parana River. Even that doesn't matter, Jake thought. St. Urbain's Horseman will take him by surprise, gaining the advantage.* (3)

This sonorous calling out of exotic names as Jake fantasizes the Horseman coming ever closer to the secluded place where Mengele believes himself to be safe, gives Jake as much satisfaction as the thought of the Horseman's actually arriving to mete out biblical justice. Since gold fillings were extracted from murdered Jews, the Horseman will extract the gold fillings from Mengele's mouth with deliberate slowness. As the latrine scene stands for countless humiliations, so the gold filling extraction represents the many hideous operations performed by Mengele and others under his command.

> *Sometimes Jake wondered if the <u>Doktor</u> given his declining years, slept with his mouth open, slack, or was it (more characteristically, perhaps) always clamped shut? Doesn't matter. In any event, the Horseman would extract the gold fillings from the triangular cleft between his upper front teeth with pliers. Slowly…* (3)

Picturing the Horseman as a kind of stealthy Jewish dentist operating on an elderly, possibly uncooperative, patient preserves the irony with which the whole Horseman enterprise is imbued. The Horseman will cleanse the world of Nazi "filth" as Hercules washed out the Augean stables—a huge task. And since Hercules also (as his eleventh labor) stole three golden apples from the Garden of the Hesperides, so the Horseman will steal the golden fillings from Mengeles' teeth.

On a higher symbolic level, Richler identifies his Horseman as one of the thirty-six just men (*Lamed-Vav Tzaddikim* in Hebrew) who—according to Jewish tradition—rise up in every generation to fight evil and injustice, and on whose account God will not destroy the world. In Richler's epigraph to *St. Urbain's Horseman* he quotes the last stanza of W.H.

Auden's poem, "September 1939," in which the "just" are invoked as defenders of an otherwise defenseless world:

> *Defenceless under the night*
> *Our world in a stupor lies;*
> *Yet, dotted everywhere,*
> *Ironic points of light*
> *Flash out wherever the Just*
> *Exchange their messages:*
> *May I, composed like them*
> *Of Eros and of dust,*
> *Beleaguered by the same*
> *Negation and despair,*
> *Show an affirming flame.*

Since Richler's Horseman is engaged in a "search and destroy mission" against evil men, he becomes a source of light to Jake in an otherwise grim and dark world. He also becomes Jake's personal "moral editor" who prods Jake into showing "an affirming flame." But the Horseman's role as moral editor is heavily ironic in that his alter ego or everyday self—Joey Hersh—appears to be rather disreputable.

However Joey is not as bad as Jake's accountant Harry Stein who carries out his own shoddy revenge fantasies rather than merely dreaming. While Jake visualizes the intrepid Horseman riding a white horse into the jungles of Paraguay searching for Mengele and fighting against forces of chaos and destruction, Harry Stein—a shifty chap who is not only Jake's accountant but also his blackmailer—fiddles tax returns for the rich and renowned. In his recreation time he takes pornographic photographs and blackmails the clients whose wealth he has preserved. Dirty Harry is, like Jake, filled with vengeful fantasies although they are of a different sort; but unlike Jake he goes out himself to avenge his perceived wrongs. Because of certain similarities in their inner lives, although their outer circumstances are very different, Jake at first develops a sneaking sympathy for Harry. And it is only when Harry almost succeeds in dragging him down into the cesspool where he lives, that Jake shakes himself free.

Jake's sympathy for Harry Stein—worked out on the subterranean level of latrines and sewage—is also revealed in an "inter-novel" word game that Richler plays with Harry's surname. In *The Apprenticeship of Duddy Kravitz*—a novel that Richler had based on Budd Schulberg's *What Makes Sammy Run?*—Duddy was modeled to some extent on Sammy, whose original surname was "Glickstein." But when Sammy grew up he dropped the "Stein" (which means "stone") from his name because he felt it slowed him down. He retained the "Glick" which means "luck" and thereafter climbed unencumbered up the slippery ladder of his tarnished success. To show that Harry Stein is the unlucky blood brother to Sammy Glick—or, to change the metaphor, cut from the same cloth—Richler gives him the second half of Sammy's surname (the "Stein" that Sammy rejected), and does not favor him with any "Glick" at all. Because of the "Stein" hanging around his neck, Harry—although as clever, devious, and amoral as Sammy—will not succeed. He cannot climb out of the slime that is his natural abode: he can only try to drag others in.

The trouble begins when Harry tries to shake down Jake who unexpectedly responds with friendly interest instead of revulsion or fear. Hooked by Harry's complaint that he is "not getting enough"—a complaint that Jake secretly shares—he makes Harry his "righteousness project." He tries to compensate Harry for a miserable childhood in London during World War II when Harry scurried like a rat in London's underground air-raid shelters while Jake lived safely in Canada.

Because of his happy marriage and successful career, Jake feels that he has missed out on certain deeper challenges and more thrilling adventures. In his middle-aged state of anxiety he asks himself, "Is this all?" Is there nothing more to look forward to? Cushioned from harsh reality by his wealth and position, restrained from new sexual conquests by the love and respect he feels for his wife, Jake ponders the irony of his fate:

> ...as long as he had been unhappy with Carol, there were others.
> Each girl a poss.
> There was also the tantalizing, all but impossible hope, of an ideal woman, Beautiful,
> Intelligent, Understandin[g]
> Now he had her. Wonderful. But cutting off the quest
> Hell, he was only 37, he could have done with another bad marriage first, thrashing from bed to bed, looking for fulfillment, lushing, complaining
> as things stood, this was it, everything,
> he had no right to expect more
> and so, is this all, is there no more to it. (Working Notes to *St. Urbain's Horseman,* University of Calgary Library Archives)

Richler's working notes emphasize what the novel implies. Jake is restless and dissatisfied with himself, envying his divorced friends who are once more on the prowl. Jake is also convinced he is a coward. He fears getting old, getting sick, losing the love of his wife. He worries that something will happen to his children. And for the first time in Richler's novels a main character modeled on the author tortures himself with thoughts of Jewish suffering, especially in the German concentration camps. Richler comes up with a number of ingenious ways to combat Jake's worries and painful thoughts. On the level of language he tries to flush the pain out of Jake's mind through the symbolic power of toilet imagery. Since Jake's name evokes a lavatory, when relatives call him to account for his behavior, his retort is "Flush, flush."

Trying to stem his secret longing to occasionally go "thrashing from bed to bed" as he had done in his premarital youth, gets Jake into serious trouble—not because of anything he does himself but because of the way he decides to help Harry. To this end he lends Harry his house while Jake and his family are away. On returning a day early he finds Harry and a young woman engaged in activities that to Jake are morally repulsive. He throws the girl out of the house; she tells the police that both Harry and Jake have violated her in ways that in Britain at the time landed people in jail. The police charge Jake and Harry with criminal behavior, and Jake faces a jail sentence beside which his other troubles begin to seem minor.

While Harry muddies the waters and drags them both down, Jake continues to elaborate fantasies of the Horseman whom he had molded from the person of his older cousin and childhood idol, Joey Hersh. Cousin Joey was strong, handsome, rebellious, and the only one Jake knew who rode a horse. Beautiful women were drawn to him—several, in spite of having husbands—and others who gave him money. He was said to be associated with organized crime. His watchword when anyone complained of injustice was "What are you going to do about it?" As an adult, he fought in the Spanish Civil War and later helped to liberate Jerusalem. Jake revered his cousin's strength, rebelliousness, and willingness to fight. In time he made Joey his moral editor and at some point transfigured him into the courageous, magnetic, Horseman of his own private Apocalypse.

> *And I saw heaven opened, and behold a white horse; and he that sat upon him was called Faithful and True, and in righteousness he doth judge and make war. (Revelation 20:11)*

In Jake's fevered imagination, Cousin Joey—like the Apocalyptic Horseman of *Revelation*—rides to battle on a white horse, judging and punishing evil doers, roaming the world to bring the wicked to judgment. But unlike the Christian Horseman who will appear only at the end of time, Jake's Horseman is riding now; smiting enemies of the Jews with his conquering sword; searching them out no matter where they might hide. Also unlike the Christian Horseman, Jake's heroic rider never relinquishes his all too human side. Joey's ex-wives and Jake's uncles insist that Joey is a bully, a bigamist, and a sexual predator who takes money from women. He is also a careless man who never bothers to pay his debts.

Jake admires Joey in spite of his flaws and never quite believes the allegations are true. He sees Joey as one of the just, the righteous, for whose sake the world will not be destroyed. He defends Joey's reputation, pays his debts, and comforts his many wives—all the while holding fast to his vision of the Horseman riding his white stallion, appearing wherever and whenever a defender is needed most.

Jake's life—even aside from his belief in the Horseman—is full of contradictions. He is named after a toilet but is chronically constipated and can't, so to speak, "go." He owns a saddle (Joey's saddle) although he cannot ride; he is being paid for a film he is not allowed to make; and he is charged with a crime he did not commit. As Jacob his name recalls the third Patriarch of Israel, but as Jake he functions like a one-man sewage system trying to flush out the clotted horrors of Jewish suffering.

At the beginning of *St. Urbain's Horseman,* Jake is in deep personal trouble, staggering under a heavy load of guilt for the world's pain that he can do nothing about. In a misplaced moment of empathy, and in an attempt to level out the British class system, he befriends the repulsive Harry Stein who lives at the lower end of the class structure. Although he picks a dangerous person to help, and pays a heavy price for his kindness, the fact that he does not let Harry down during their trial on criminal sex charges satisfies his personal code of honor. At the end of the story, after Jake wins his case and is set free, he receives a letter telling him that his cousin Joey has been killed in a plane crash—which means that the Horseman can no longer ride. Still numb from the funeral of his father from which he has just returned, and at which he found himself unable to cry, Jake weeps uncontrollably at the news of his cousin's death.

> *What are you going to do about it, a voice demanded.*
> *He wept, that's what. The tears he couldn't coax out of himself at his father's graveside or summon up for Mr. Justice Beal's verdict on Harry or his mother's departure flowed freely. Torn from his soul, the tears welled in his throat and ran down his cheeks. He whimpered, he moaned. He sank trembling to the sofa. He wept for his*

> father,…rotting in an oversize pinewood casket. He wept for his mother who deserved a more loving son. He wept for Harry, fulminating in his cell and assuredly planning vengeance…. He wept because the Horseman, his conscience, his mentor, was no more. (464)

As Jake's tears sluice away his sorrow, he contemplates taking on the role of Horseman himself. He privately admits that he might have been worshipping a false God—one he had fashioned out of his own needs as the biblical Aaron created a Golden Calf. When he finds out that Joey's gun is merely a stage prop, shooting blanks, Jake calms down. Although he decides to consider the Horseman only "presumed dead," we understand that a certain phase in Jake's life is over and that he is now free to contemplate something new.

For Richler, the writing of *St. Urbain's Horseman* signifies that he has "done something" for his people. He has borne witness. He has shown an affirming flame. And now he is ready to leave England and return home to Canada, to Montreal—a perilous homecoming that will be fictionalized in his next novel, *Joshua Then and Now*. Cousin Joey, the Horseman's human counterpart, had changed his name as he moved from country to country. For a while he was an actor in Germany where he called himself Jesse Hope—a suitable name in that the Horseman always represented hope rather than reality. The Thirty Six Just Men, who are supposed to rise up in every generation so that God will not destroy the world, may also be merely the hope of pious men. There may not be a network of ironic points of light protecting us from harm. Nevertheless, to "show an affirming flame" is always a good thing to do. And shoveling trouble—in the stables of a God in whom he cannot bring himself to believe—is one of Richler's special gifts.

Joshua Then and Now: Bridging the Gap

The river flowed both ways. The current moved from north to south, but the wind usually came from the south, rippling the bronze-green water in the opposite direction. This apparently impossible contradiction, made apparent and possible, still fascinated Morag, even after years of river-watching. (Margaret Laurence, The Diviners, 3)

Morag returned to the house, to write the remaining private and fictional words, and to set down her title. (The Diviners, 453)

In her last novel, *The Diviners*, Margaret Laurence (who had returned to Canada after many years abroad) writes the life-story of a writer who has come to the end of her talent, and knows that in the area of fiction she has nothing left to say. Laurence calls the opening chapter of her book, "River of Now and Then."

In his seventh novel, Mordecai Richler—returning to Canada after many years abroad—wittily inverts Laurence's chapter heading to create his own title: *Joshua Then and Now*. In keeping with the title, he writes a "Time is a river that flows both ways" novel himself. Because his earlier books had flowed out quite quickly and he now needs more and more time between each novel, Richler shares Laurence's anxiety, worrying that his literary well has run dry, that he no longer has anything worthwhile to write about.

Laurence's premonition sadly turned out to be true. In the twelve years between *The Diviners* and her death, she wrote no more novels. But Richler's fears fortunately were false. In the years between *Joshua Then and Now* and the end of his life he produced the marvelously inventive, intricately plotted *Solomon Gursky Was Here*, before closing with his triumphantly ironic elegy, *Barney's Version*.

Still, in 1972 when Richler came back to Canada to live, he was filled with apprehension. Like Laurence he had spent productive years building his literary reputation away from home. He had—again like Laurence—received two Governor General's Awards for his novels, and had, like Laurence, seen one of his novels, *The Apprenticeship of Duddy Kravitz*, made into a successful film. Both Richler and Laurence had married and divorced; both were raising a family but again Richler was luckier, returning to Canada with a much-loved second wife.

Looking back to years of achievement and forward to an uncertain future, Richler had good reason to gaze into the river of then and now with alarm, wondering what might lie ahead. But unlike Laurence, who watched the river from her cottage on its banks, Richler built a bridge to take him safely across. From that bridge, which he called *Joshua Then and Now* (and critics immediately dubbed "Mordecai Then and Now"), he could look down on that tricky river of time while still moving steadily ahead.

Joshua Then and Now is, above all, a novel of transition. It flows between Joshua's and Richler's present past, distant past, and biblical ancestry—all the while moving toward a future embodying their hopes and dreams. This bridge of memory and desire, along which Joshua leads his intrepid band of Shapiros, is filled with peril at every step. Joshua must fight unfinished battles from the past even as new troubles rise up to meet him. And he must keep his eyes and heart fixed steadfastly on the land he is journeying toward, the place he wants to be when the current battles are over.

As in *Son of a Smaller Hero* where he uses the biblical precedent of Noah and the Ark to support his own sailing away, Richler again turns to the Bible for ironic justification. This time he chooses the story of Joshua leading the Israelites over the River Jordan and into the Promised Land—a story of many battles with Canaanites, Amorites, and other tribes inhabiting the land that the Israelites now considered to be their own.

So Richler leads his band of Richlers and Josh Shapiro leads his band of Shapiros across the water from England to Canada. Both Richler and Joshua have to fight to re-establish themselves in the land of their birth—a country (Canada) and a city (Montreal) that they had gladly left behind many years before. In the Bible, Joshua leads the Israelites into the Promised Land only after Moses has died. For Mordecai Richler, it is only after the death of his father, Moses Isaac Richler, that he is able to go home and write a going-home novel.

When the biblical Joshua brought down the walls of Jericho and marched into Canaan with his twelve tribes of Israel, the first tribe was named Reuben. In Richler's novel, Josh Shapiro's father—at one time a boxer and another time an enforcer for the mob—fights enthusiastically at his son's side when Josh has scores to settle. While his son was still a small boy, Reuben Shapiro proved that he was also a surprisingly gifted, idiosyncratic interpreter of the Bible, teaching morality to Josh in the form of "sex-and-religion" lectures that are a comic highlight of the book.

Reuben's biblical parodies are Richler's way of acknowledging, and at the same time mocking, his reliance on the Bible as background for his contemporary "coming home" novel. But Reuben's boxing talents come from a non-biblical source: the real-life story of a famous Jewish boxer: Reuben Goldstein known in his day as "Ruby, Jewel of the Ghetto." However, Reuben Shapiro's tender and protective love for his son, his biblical expertise, and his mighty hand, make him the wonderful father that the author of *Joshua Then and Now* could only conjure up after his own father had died. Always writing about fathers "more sinned against than sinning" while Moses Richler was alive, his son only felt free after his death to give his protagonist a father nearer to his own heart's desire.

In his essay "My Father's Life," Richler expresses sorrow at his own father's diminished existence:

> *Moses Isaac Richler*
> *Insufficient straw, NO SUCCESS was the story of his life. Neither of his marriages really worked. There were searing quarrels with my older brother. As a boy I made life difficult for him. I had no respect. Later, officious strangers would rebuke him in the synagogue for the novels I had written. Heaping calumny on the Jews, they said. If there was such a thing as a reverse Midas touch, he had it. Not one of my father's penny mining stocks ever went into orbit. He lost regularly at gin rummy. As younger, more intrepid brothers and cousins began to prosper, he assured my mother, "The bigger they come, the harder they fall."*
> *My mother, her eyes charged with scorn, laughed in his face. "You're the eldest and what are you? Nothing." (Home Sweet Home, 1984, 57-8)*

Unlike the father in *Son of a Smaller Hero*—who painfully repeats Moses Richler's failures including the bad marriage and wifely disrespect; or the father in *The Apprenticeship of Duddy Kravitz*—who until the very end shrugs off Duddy's attempts to gain his love; Reuben Shapiro has an adoring wife and an unabashed tenderness for his son. Although after his boxing career he lives to some extent outside the law, and the furniture with which he lovingly fills Joshua's house is "hot," Reuben is exactly the kind of father that Joshua needs. Moreover, although he has retired from active criminal activities by the time Joshua returns to Montreal, his former exploits come in handy when he and Joshua plan their last escapade, freeing Joshua from the blackmail of a crooked cop.

In this and other schemes he cooks up to protect his son, Reuben has a loyal co-conspirator, Senator Stephen Andrew Hornby, the aristocratic father of Joshua's wife Pauline. The elderly former Senator matches the elderly former boxer in his sense of mischief, flexible moral standards, and fierce protectiveness toward Josh and Pauline. Thus Joshua finds himself with two fathers who see him safely through his hazardous return home.

However Joshua's mother—based on the biblical Book of Esther rather than the Book of Joshua—gives her son more headaches than help. Esther Shapiro, or Esty Blossom as she calls herself in her porno star second life, displays the sexual appetite Richler deplored in his own mother. But Josh—unlike Richler—is neither embarrassed by nor resentful of his mother's "loopy" behavior. He protects her fiercely even when she performs a fan dance strip tease at his Bar Mitzvah party. In later years, when as Esty Blossom she becomes even more outrageously promiscuous, he maintains a weary affection for which she is grateful. When Josh himself is disgraced she proclaims her loyalty by marching around with placards proclaiming his innocence. Of all Richler's fictional mothers, Esther Shapiro has the best relationship with her son. He adores her in his youth and still cares for her—in spite of her scandalous behavior—when he is middle-aged. By being the total antithesis of Jake Hersh's guilt-inducing mother in *St. Urbain's Horseman*, Esty Blossom wins her son's heart, and the reader's as well.

But of course it is by her beauty, sex appeal, and strength of purpose that Esther Shapiro becomes a parody of that Queen Esther who in the Book of Esther saved thousands of Persian Jews from being massacred. The Bible story tells us that Ahasuerus, King of Persia, wanted to show his beautiful first wife Vashti to his assembled nobles, and he was furious when she refused to appear. Putting her aside (which seems to have been easy to do in those days, at least for kings), he set up a contest in which the most beautiful virgins of Persia would compete to become his new wife. Esther's uncle Mordecai entered her in the contest, and her beauty so dazzled the King that he immediately married her.

But while the King was occupied with beauty contests and marriage, Haman, the King's evil Prime Minister, decided to put all the Jews of Persia to death so that he could confiscate their property to enrich himself and the king. He also decided to have Esther's uncle Mordecai hanged for not showing Haman the proper respect. However, unbeknownst to Haman, Mordecai had recently overheard a plot against the King's life which was foiled with his help. And Ahasuerus was planning to give Mordecai a big reward. When Mordecai discovered Haman's murderous and larcenous plans, he instructed Esther to go to the King and use her wiles to save him and all her people. Esther approached the King even though it was strictly forbidden to do so without being sent for, and she "found favor in his sight." Ravished by her beauty and her charm, Ahasuerus swore she could have anything she wished, even half his kingdom. Because of Esther's intervention, Haman was hanged on his own gallows and the Jews of Persia were saved. Mordecai was made Prime Minister in Haman's place and the Jews were allowed to revenge themselves against the Persian people.

This is not exactly how Reuben Shapiro tells the story to his son. In a mocking parody of the Book of Esther (and an ironic travesty of Richler's first name), Reuben calls Esther's uncle Mordecai "a real conniver, a suckhole, a very bloodthirsty fella...and certainly the first Jewish pimp." He portrays Esther as a skilled wanton "planted inside [the palace] screwing the royal head off every night," and allowing her uncle to use her in his own political game. In Reuben's version, Mordecai's ultimate purpose was to become Prime Minister and to revenge himself on the man who sought his life.

> *Not only is Haman hanging on the gallows he set up for Mordecai, but the king now turns around and grants the right to the Jews, quote, to destroy, to slay, and to cause to perish, all the power of the people...both little ones and women, and to take the spoil of them for prey, unquote....Mordecai and his followers they kill seventy-five thousand enemies, men, women, and children, which is why we celebrate Purim, quote a day of feasting and gladness, unquote.* (290-91)

Reuben's version of the Purim story suggests that Mordecai Richler—sensitive about his name and aware of his own vengeful nature—mocks himself and the mother who bore and named him. He savages the Story of Esther and the uncle who sent her to save the Jews by seducing the king with her sexual charms. He also suggests that the Jews—celebrating with feasting and gladness a devastating slaughter of men women and children—are no better than the Persians who were ready to do the same to them. In this way Richler causes us to rethink an old Bible story and the festival of Purim that flows from it. We are led to wonder what moral lessons such a story is meant to display.

Joshua Then and Now is filled with vengeful attacks on supposed enemies, and these assaults finally bring Joshua to a ludicrous state of physical collapse. While trying to flee from police after his latest escapade, his car crashes because the brakes (which he had forgotten to have repaired) fail. When the book begins, Joshua is not leading twelve tribes of Israelites into the Promised Land, he is lying in a hospital bed contemplating the twelve alien pints of blood being pumped into his veins to keep him alive.

> *Look at me now, Joshua thought. His right leg was no longer suspended by pulleys from a hospital ceiling, but it was still held in a cast, multiple fractures healing slowly at his age. There were no more tubes unwinding out of his nostrils or feeding him intravenously or draining his lungs. Lungs bubbling with blood whenever he took a breath. Yet he continued to brood about all the blood they had pumped into him. Twelve alien pints. It flooded his dreams, it polluted his waking hours. The odds were that some of the blood had been peddled to the hospital by winos or junkies. I'm bound to come down with hepatitis, he thought. Worse maybe.* (1)

As Joshua lies shattered in a hospital bed, his wife, who has already suffered an emotional collapse, unaccountably disappears. On top of these misfortunes, Joshua's masculinity is being seriously questioned because of a reckless, generous act of brotherly love, and a pseudo-salacious literary correspondence (undertaken in fun) suddenly surfaces, leaving him open to blackmail. Every aspect of Joshua's life is now in shambles, giving him ample reason to look back at his "then" so that he can begin to make sense of his "now."

Joshua's "then" involved growing-up in the care of his sexy, resentful mother while his father hid out from the police, gangsters, or both. At that time Joshua shied away from his father's love, and did not appreciate his "Sex and the Bible" lessons. Later in Joshua's "then" came his flawed idyll on the Spanish island of Ibiza where the former Nazi with his double doctorate—Dr. Dr. Mueller—set him up for blackmail and questioned his manhood: "Are you a man or a mouse?" Later still came Joshua's successful courtship of the still-married Pauline, followed by their happy marriage, growing family, and successful years in London. Finally, in the "then" but verging on the "now" came the return to Canada and Montreal, and Pauline's painful re-entry into her Westmount and Lake Memphremagog social crowd, with Joshua too busy fighting his own battles to be able to help Pauline with hers. Then suddenly these battles ended, pitching Joshua into his present state, lying in a hospital bed, shattered in body and soul, lost without Pauline, smack in the middle of his "now."

Yet Joshua's "now" is not static. Slowly, as his battle wounds heal and he works out the dynamics of where he has been and where he is now, he begins to plan new campaigns, this time with the aid of his father's and father-in-law's ingenious assistance. By this time Joshua has only two goals: to lure Pauline back home, and to entrap the police officer who is trying to blackmail him. When the book ends, both goals are about to be met. But the soft focus happy ending, no less than the hard-edged battles all serve the purpose of Richler's parody. He is writing a "time is a river that flows both ways" kind of novel while at the same time, making fun of what he is doing. Josh Shapiro's "then" does not really explain his "now"; nor do the many battles fought by his biblical predecessor make his own vengefulness any less ridiculous.

Like his author, Joshua has a powerful and idiosyncratic moral code. Willing to follow at least eight of the Ten Commandments without believing in the God who cast them in stone, he is not surprised to find himself the helpless object of (this perhaps non-existent) God's wrath. Neither is he astonished when, at the end of the novel, at least some of his losses are restored. Looked at from this angle, the novel seems to be adding a bit of a parody on the Book of Job to the theme of Joshua fighting his way into the Promised Land. In neither the story of Job's God-sanctioned, guiltless sufferings, nor the story of Joshua's God-commanded, wholesale slaughters does God come off very well.

In the Book of Job, Satan wagers with God that if Job loses everything he owns, he will "curse God and die." God wagers that Job will remain faithful in spite of being tormented. In the Book of Joshua, when it comes to Joshua's entering the Promised Land, God commands him to put to the sword every man, woman, and child belonging to the tribes that come against him. This seems rather excessive of God, and of the fighter who obeys His command. As Reuben's biblical lectures imply that Bible stories do not necessarily teach clear moral lessons, so Richler's giving his characters biblical names does not imply that examples from the Bible should be uncritically followed. By beginning his novel with Josh Shapiro lying in a hospital bed with his body and reputation in tatters, Richler seems to be teaching a moral lesson of his own: in spite of a multitude of biblical examples, taking vengeance into one's own hands is a dangerous affair.

Although Josh Shapiro's catastrophic losses remind us of the tribulations of Job, Josh's situation is at least partly his own fault; and his salvation will depend to a large extent on himself as well. Even though the pattern of sin, punishment, and redemption in *Joshua Then and Now* are fiction, the events in Joshua's life are clearly modeled on Richler's own. This includes the time Richler spent on the Spanish island of Ibiza as a young man, where he met several ex-Nazis, took part in local orgies, had a heated romance, and got into trouble with the police. It also reflects his return to the island twenty-five years later to find that everything and everyone had changed. While Joshua accomplishes nothing by returning to Ibiza and leaving Pauline to face her problems alone, Richler's second visit to the island, accompanied by his wife, provides him with material for the eighth novel.

As Richler and Joshua navigate the river dividing "then" from "now," both show themselves to be "splendid, promiscuous haters"; but both also bestow on certain friends an unstinting, unquestioning love. True friends can do no wrong, while "presumed enemies" can do no right. The two men (aside from his father and father-in-law) closest to Joshua's heart, the friends he protects without any thought of danger to himself, are Murdoch and Seymour. Childish, vulgar, deceitful, each is the type of friend that W.H. Auden celebrates in the poem, "Lay your sleeping head my love": the first stanza of which Richler chose as epigraph to the book.

By sleeping on the floor in Murdoch's hotel room after his sick friend has thoroughly disgraced himself and by kissing Murdoch on the mouth in front of shocked onlookers, Joshua demonstrates his loyalty and love. Although the love is entirely platonic, it is understandably misunderstood. And Richler's use of W.H. Auden's celebration of gay love as epigraph to a story that carries love between "straight" men to ridiculous extremes, shows that he is being deliberately provocative. When Joshua's friend Seymour—who has begun wearing black silk panties to embarrass himself out of yielding to the charms of any woman other than his wife—nevertheless yields to temptation, he asks Joshua to exchange underwear with him so that he can bed a seductive girl. Joshua makes the exchange and catastrophe promptly follows.

Although his devotion to old friends leaves him open to blackmail and ridicule, Joshua, in his admittedly exaggerated way, demonstrates the courage it takes to be a brother to other men. This is something that Andre Bennet, Richler's hero in *The Acrobats,* held up as an ideal but did not live long enough to carry out. By showing Joshua to be a true brother to his friends, Richler indicates that this ideal is still one of the flames he holds high. Being Richler, however, he cannot resist pushing the convention of brotherly love into the realm of parody.

In *St. Urbain's Horseman*, Richler's first kick at his own mid-life crisis, the central questions were: "Is this all there is?" and more importantly: "What are you going to do about it?" Jacob Hersh's response was to try to balance out some of the inequities of the British social system. Richler's response was "to bear witness" through his writing—to the atrocities of the holocaust and the often unbearable inequities of everyday life, and thereby "show an affirming flame."

In *Joshua Then and Now*, a still unresolved mid-life crisis is complicated by the return of Richler—and his surrogate Joshua Shapiro—to the unfinished business of their youth and the family and friends they left behind. Tying his hero to the biblical Joshua who led the Israelites into the Promised Land, fighting and destroying all who lived there at the time, Richler sets up a war situation that his hero has to resolve. Josh Shapiro has to fight the established Westmount and Lake Memphremagog elite to carve out a space for himself and his little tribe of Shapiros. He has to confront family and friends who denigrate the literary reputation he earned abroad, while they made their fortunes at home. He has to deal with his mother's promiscuity and the helpless love he nevertheless feels for her. He has to earn his formidable father-in-law's respect, and loosen his wife's semi-incestuous attachment to her failed "golden-boy" brother. He has to stop the former friends of his youth from moving in on his beautiful wife.

The title of Richler's book, *Joshua Then and Now,* leads us to expect (as in Margaret Laurence's *Diviners*) a clear pattern of events starting with the hero's childhood and continuing until his present age and situation in the "now" of the book. But Richler confounds all such expectations. Not only are the childhood and adult memories distributed in random ways, but the big return to Montreal after many years abroad is complicated by another return, this time to Ibiza, where Joshua must finally come to terms with other changes that time has wrought. He goes to fight a return match with

Dr. Dr. Mueller whose double doctorate (medical degree and Ph.D) symbolized his double superiority over Joshua—in age and worldly success. But Mueller is dead; Joshua's thirst for revenge is left unsatisfied; and back in Montreal Pauline is rapidly falling apart. Leaving the home front undefended while going abroad to fight a stupid old battle proves to be a tactical error resulting in almost irreparable harm. In the interim "now" of Joshua's life, both he and Pauline are in hospital suffering in body and mind.

And yet by the end of the book Joshua is on his way to recovery, nursed and protected by his father and father-in-law who break all sorts of biblical commandments to keep him safe. And Pauline has tentatively ventured home, hopefully to live with Joshua "happily ever after." Since fighting of one kind or another constitutes the main action in *Joshua Then and Now*, the domestic scene at the end signals that a hero, bloodied and broken in battle, is entitled to the comfort of his wife's arms. He may also, without dishonor, accept the help of older veterans who keep his enemies away while he mends in body and soul. In this novel, Richler mocks many things including himself, his parents, the revenge tradition, the Bible, the retrospective novel, and the difficulty of returning home. But he treats with great tenderness the love between man and wife, the loyalty a man owes his friends, and the devotion between parent and child. Richler's turbulent "River of Now and Then" flows backward to his accomplished past and forward to a future still unknown. But we his readers know that his future includes two magnificent novels—driven like this one by equal parts of rage and love.

Solomon Gursky Was Here: Biography as Quest

> *Strong and Never Wrong is He*
> *Worthy of our song is He,*
> *Never Failing,*
> *All prevailing,*
> *Built the Temple in our days.*
> *Speedily, O speedily,*
> *Built that all may sing Thy praise.*
> (227)

    Only the capitalized pronouns tell us that this song—sung by Ephraim Gursky in the British coal mines where he toiled at the age of eleven—is meant to be in praise of God, and not in praise of the mighty King Solomon who built the first Temple in Jerusalem. And a deliberate blurring of qualities pertaining to God and to man occurs regularly in this most audacious and intricate of Richler's novels.

    In a story packed with vivid personalities—each of whom tracks his own unique path—Ephraim Gursky and Solomon, his "chosen grandson," stand apart. While everyone else, for better or worse, lives only one life, Ephraim and Solomon shed their skins and emerge renewed to live again and again—in Solomon's case, each time with a different name. They are shape-changers like the Raven who serves as their emblem and their friend. And like the mischievous raven who, in the mythology of many nations, is said to be able to change from bird to man and back again performing supernatural deeds, Ephraim and Solomon lead a magical, God-like existence. Solomon Gursky—after the plane crash in the

Canadian frozen North that was thought to have killed him—reappears in London as Baron Corvo, and later makes other appearances under other names. Ephraim Gursky as a young lad miraculously walks away from the doomed Franklin Expedition of 1845: he and a Jewish doctor being the sole survivors. Their miraculous survival is attributed to having brought kosher food on board rather than eating from the regular crew's tainted tins. Ephraim and Izzy (the doctor) walk into an Inuit camp, and after performing several pseudo-scientific feats that astonish the tribe, Ephraim declares himself their leader and their God, thereby creating a new tribe of Ephraim in the Northern Kingdom of Canada.

> *And Ephraim said unto them:*
> *"I am Ephraim, the Lord thy God, and thou shalt have no other gods before me.*
> *"Thou shalt not bow down to Narssuk…or to any other god….For the Lord thy God is a jealous God, visiting the iniquity of the fathers upon the children unto the third and fourth generation of them that hate me."…*
> *"Six days shalt thou hunt, providing meat for me and Izzy, and on the evening of the sixth day thou shalt wash thy women and bring them to me, an offering."*(439)

By pre-empting and rearranging the Ten Commandments and by sowing his seed liberally among his recently converted followers, Ephraim establishes himself and his house in the frozen North. When later in life he begets a European son whom he names "Aaron" and brings out to the Canadian West, Ephraim begets the non-Inuit House of Gursky. This flourishing offshoot of Ephraim's family becomes—in the words of one reviewer—"a Canadian branch of the House of Israel."

Like Ephraim his grandfather, Solomon Gursky is fond of appropriating God's words. When questioned about his new identity after the supposedly fatal plane crash, Solomon grandly proclaims: "I am that I am" which in the Bible is God's answer to Moses from the Burning Bush. The name "Solomon" is of course meant to remind us of the biblical King

Solomon, famous for his wisdom and believed to have written the erotic "Song of Songs" as well as the philosophical "Book of Ecclesiastes." By his wisdom, his wealth, his women, and his literary works, Solomon Gursky is a worthy namesake.

In the Bible, Ephraim occupies less space than King Solomon, but was important as head of the Tribe of Ephraim that occupied the Northern Kingdom when Israel was divided into North and South, which happened about three thousand years ago. According to tradition, God declared: "I am father to Israel and Ephraim is my first born." *(Jeremiah 31:9)* Actually Ephraim was the second son but received the first son's blessing. This was to signify that his descendants would become a mightier people than those of his brother (a fact pointed out to Ephraim Gursky by Mr. Nicholson who was his language teacher, seducer, and friend when Ephraim was a young man). Since the name "Ephraim" means "fruitful," Richler riffs on the meaning of the name by having Ephraim Gursky scatter his seed far and wide in Europe and Canada. He becomes patriarch to the Gursky family after first impregnating various Inuit tribes in the far North. These northern tribes imprinted with his name are ever after known as Gor-ski, Girskee, Gur-ski, and Goorsky.

The narrator of Richler's novel is a character as crucial to the plot as the Gurskys with whom he is obsessed. His name is "Moses," like the Old Testament Moses who was thought to have written early Jewish history in the first five books of the Bible. Richler's Moses Berger takes up the story of early Jewish life in Canada, epitomized by the opening up of the liquor trade in the West by his fictional Gursky family. The biblical Moses supposedly wrote under the direction of God, whose voice he could hear but whose face he was not allowed to see. So Moses Berger writes under the direction of God-like Solomon Gursky—an all-knowing, all-powerful surrogate father who appears to Moses Berger without being recognized, and then does not appear again. Yet he never ceases to watch over his surrogate son—guiding, guarding, and inspiring him—while Moses writes the Gursky family history from its promising rise to its sordid decline.

When Moses Berger, already obsessed with the Gursky family, wonders how to go about writing his story, a beautiful old woman, sadly crippled by polio, comes into his life. The elegant Mrs. McClure—once the lover of Solomon Gursky—steers Moses toward a distinctive method of writing biography. She recommends the book that Richler used as template for the novel in which Moses Berger and Mrs. McClure appear: "If I may be so presumptuous, I think an excellent model for you might be *The Quest for Corvo* by A.J.A. Symons. Brilliant, I thought."(394)

The Quest for Corvo (1934) is fascinating to read at any time, but doubly exciting after reading *Solomon Gursky Was Here*. It so clearly gives Richler the paradigm for a biography in which the biographer's feelings, thoughts, and experiences are as important, and take up as much space, as the subject of his biography. Furthermore it supplies the Raven symbol that Richler adopts and parodies as the leitmotif of his book.

Subtitled *An Experimental Biography*, Symons' book shows how he first hears about the writer/painter/failed priest/and amazingly self-destructive Frederick William Rolfe. After reading some of Rolfe's books and hearing certain things about the way Rolfe lived, Symons devotes more and more of his own life to the pursuit of his increasingly elusive subject, sharing with his readers all aspects of the rough and ragged search. He relates how he came to be interested in the man whose life and work he gathers with such passionate determination and care. He details every scrap of information that comes his way and all the methods he uses to ferret out those who might have had contact with Rolfe when he was alive. He admits to having many unanswered questions at the end of his quest and leaves the mystery of Rolfe's life largely unsolved.

When Richler takes on the challenge of writing a fictionalized biography of a certain well-known Montreal family, he parodies Symons' format by taking it to extremes. He first appropriates the Raven symbol and then weaves it into Solomon Gursky's many disguises and activities. Since Frederick Rolfe had used "Baron Corvo" as his primary nom de plume, Solomon Gursky—after his supposedly fatal plane crash—calls himself "Baron Corvo." Solomon then appears as Mr. Corbeau "the naturalist from California" (327); Mr. Cuervo "a dealer in Kikuyu and Masai antiquities...[with] a gallery on...Rodeo Drive"(541); and Herr Dr. Otto Raven "a little Swiss Banker." (518). Solomon is the shadowy genius behind Corvus Trust of Zurich and a major shareholder of the Raven Mine in Yellowknife. He owns mythological paintings of ravens, plants a stuffed raven on his brother Bernard's grave, and at the end of the novel flies north in a plane that turns into "a raven with flapping wings."

Symons' book provides a helpful gloss on Richler's multilingual adaptation of the raven name:

> *It may just be noted in passing that the title which the Baron selected is of the following signification—Latin, corvus; Italian, corvo; French corbeau; Scotch, corbie; English, crow.*
> [note] this...is inaccurate; corvus is raven, not crow; and it was the raven that Baron Corvo took as his emblem. (*Quest*, 32)

Symons learned that Rolfe—as Baron Corvo—stamped all his personal belongings with the raven crest and kept a stuffed raven in a place of honor at his table. Richler takes this stuffed raven to new heights (or depths) when a stuffed raven is found planted on the evil Bernard Gursky's grave as a curse that will follow him into the world beyond. Ravens are totem birds for Solomon and Ephraim, serving as their signature, their helpers and friends. When a foolish hunter shoots one of Ephraim's birds, the hunter is found hanging under baffling circumstances the following day.

Without knowing that Richler's ravens flew out of Symons' *Quest for Corvo,* readers still find the recurring motif highly entertaining. But we chuckle more appreciatively when we see where the idea originated and how limited it was before Richler performed his magic: first anchoring it firmly in "Eskimo" lore and then swelling its flight with the breadth of his imagination. For the "good guys" Richler's ravens show themselves to be friends and familiars, but for the "bad guys" and those who are about to make a terrible mistake they are signs and portents of doom.

However, variations on the raven theme make up only a part of Richler's debt to Symons' *Quest for Corvo*. The main focus in both Symons' and Richler's books is on a writer intrigued by, and for much of his life obsessed with, the life and works of an extraordinary, multi-talented man. In Symons' biography this man was Frederick William Rolfe and he was real, although for much of his life he pretended to be someone else. The quest in Symons's book was conducted by the author and he writes in his own voice all the way through. By contrast, in Richler's novel both the narrator and Solomon Gursky are fictional, although Moses Berger is a parodic version of Richler writing this particular book. In his parody of Symons *Quest for Corvo* Richler separates himself from a narrator who shares his own physical description and failings, his moral stance, his personality and at least some of his history. He plays "peek-a-boo" with the reader while making fun of his own obsessions, his research methods, and the Montreal family on which the Gurskys are based.

> *He had turned fifty-two a few months earlier and was not yet troubled by a paunch....He was not, as he had once hoped even unconventionally handsome. A reticent man of medium height with receding brown hair running to grey and large, slightly protuberant brown eyes, their pouches purply. His nose bulbous, his lips thick. But even now some women seemed to find his physical ugliness oddly compelling. Not so much attractive as a case to answer for.* (9)

Found right near the beginning of the novel, this description of Moses Berger perfectly matches Richler's photograph on the book's back cover, so that we cannot avoid hearing and seeing Richler whenever Moses Berger speaks. Never is this more apparent than when the middle-aged Moses contemplates his reasons for devoting the better part of his life to Solomon and the rest of the Gursky family. To explain his obsession, he uses the metaphor of his favorite salmon lure, his Silver Doctor, which he loses at the beginning of the book and regains at the end when a lady friend unexpectedly sits on it. Looking at his Silver Doctor and pondering the intimate relationship between a fisherman and the fish he is trying to catch, Moses moves on to consider the intricate, reciprocal relationship between a writer and his subject. He wonders whether he had decided to write a biography of Solomon and the Gurskys of his own free will, or whether it was the crafty Solomon who chose him to be the Gursky family scribe. By the end of the novel, Moses is so wrung out by his task that he is convinced he will never be able to write anything else again.

> *Moses sat staring at the salmon fly he had set out on the table. His Silver Doctor. After all his years on the rivers it finally struck him that he wasn't the angler but the salmon. A teasing, gleeful Solomon casting the flies over his head, getting him to roll, rise, and dance on his tail at will. Sea-bright Moses was when he first took the hook, but no more than a black salmon now, ice-bound in a dark river, the open sea closed to him.* (550)

Because of the intentional similarity in sound between salmon and Solomon, and the long fishing camp chapter that Richler inserts in the novel, we must take seriously the metaphor of a writer being caught by his subject rather than casting about for a subject on which to write. We do know that the Bronfman family of Seagram fame did not ask Richler to write a sensationalized, fictional biography—especially one that featured a God-like brother with the best qualities of Harry and Abe who had been shunted aside by Sam Bronfman in real life. We also know that they were not amused by the final result.

While Richler's imagination was clearly caught by A.J.A. Symons' *Quest for Corvo*, he was no less indebted to Peter C. Newman's *The Bronfman Dynasty*. Newman's book provided him with a detailed early Bronfman history and careful descriptions of the four brothers (Abe, Harry, Sam, and Allan) who together founded Seagram and the family fortune.

Solomon Gursky Was Here: Biography as Quest   117

> *This book attempts to document for the first time the controversial history and impressive influence of a supremely monied, infinitely complex, and highly neurotic family: the Bronfmans of Montreal and New York. Little known outside their own closed circles, they rank high among the non-Arab world's richest citizens, and their ascendancy grows daily. The mystery that has been deliberately created to shroud the Bronfmans early careers in bootlegging through Canada's West was not simple to dispel. Fortunately I managed to track down several of the surviving associates during the Bronfman brothers' adventures in the Saskatchewan liquor trade....As supporting documentation, I was able to obtain a copy of Harry Bronfman's unpublished personal account of the family's earliest days on the Prairies. I was also allowed access to some papers collected by Clifford Harvison, the RCMP corporal who arrested the Bronfman brothers in 1934 on criminal conspiracy charges.*

An introduction to *Solomon Gursky Was Here*? No. These are the opening lines of the "Author's Note" in Peter Newman's *The Bronfman Dynasty*, the unauthorized biography that tells us everything we ever wanted to know about the Bronfmans and their wealth (everything except what is hidden in their hearts). The book is even-toned and factual, giving praise to the family's determination, resourcefulness, and years of hard work. While Newman notes the harsh things Samuel Bronfman did to maintain a clear dynastic line for his own sons, and the shady practices the family engaged in during their bootlegging days, there is no rush to judgment. We find no trace of Newman's own feelings, no probing of psychological depths, no embroidering of facts.

Combining Newman's facts with Symons' method and his own satiric, judgmental temperament, Richler's novel explodes with passion, humor, ambition, jealousy, fear, and despair: all the emotions that Newman resolutely kept out of his gentlemanly account. Richler takes the basic elements that Newman provides, but gives them a wild spin of his own, adding—in keeping with his other source, Symons' *Quest For Corvo*—a deeply involved fictional biographer who is obsessed with the people he is writing about. He includes a detailed description of the way Moses Berger conducts his research, especially the bits and pieces of information he gets from various people he interviews, the books and letters he reads, and his emotional reaction to everything he uncovers. Above all, Moses Berger profits from the ghostly presence of Solomon Gursky who—in his many transformations—provides the fictional equivalent of Newman's research, including the unpublished memoirs of the almost forgotten brother, Harry Bronfman.

Published in 1978 (eleven years before Richler published *Solomon Gursky*), *The Bronfman Dynasty* is a carefully researched, deeply detailed account of individual members of the Bronfman family and the huge financial empire from its early beginnings in the Canadian West to its expansion all over the world. In a sharp departure from Newman's book and its celebration of a family's immense achievement, Richler's *Solomon Gursky* describes in intimate detail a fictionalized family's fragmentation and decline.

> *Isaac babbled to one and all about his movie-making plans and Barney was turning up on talk-shows everywhere, gabbing about his future plans for McTavish, including a bid for a major baseball franchise, and a scheme to tow icebergs from the Arctic to the Middle East.* (*Solomon Gursky*, 553)

The Gurskys begin with the lusty, gutsy, multi-talented Ephraim and his spirited, entrepreneurial young grandsons Solomon, Bernard and Morrie. The grandsons become progressively more self-serving, greedy, and dysfunctional, spawning children that are spoiled, venal, and generally nutty. Continuing to slide downward, the Gurskys display the ultimate symbol of their moral decay when the repulsive Isaac Gursky cannibalizes his father on Passover in the Arctic wilds.

Isaac's non-kosher Passover meal goes beyond the eating of an American colonel on the DEW line by Atuk in *The Incomparable Atuk*. But while Atuk is eventually guillotined in the book that bears his name, Isaac ends up as head of the Gursky liquor empire. In this episode, Richler not only parodies an event from his earlier novel, giving it a cynical twist in keeping with his attitude toward the family that his Gurskys represent, he also grotesquely inverts the biblical story of Abraham and Isaac.

In the Bible, Abraham's faith is so strong that he is ready to carry out God's command to sacrifice Isaac his only son. Only at the last minute does an angel intervene by showing Abraham a ram caught in a nearby thicket. So Abraham kills the ram instead of his son, and Abraham and Isaac go home in peace.

In Richler's parody, the story is reversed. Henry Gursky (the saintly but slightly retarded son of Solomon) has moved to the far North so that he can take care of the Jewish-Inuit descendants of his great-grandfather Ephraim. Henry's special mission is to provide his Inuit brethren with matzo for the Passover meal; and on his last trip out he takes with him his only son Isaac (as well as an Inuit boy). On their return home, the three get lost. Some time later, rescuers arrive to find that Henry and the Innuit boy are dead but Isaac is alive, having sustained himself on his father's flesh. In this reversed version of the sacrifice of Isaac, no angel intervenes to prevent the ultimate Passover travesty. And it is Isaac, along with his equally unsavory Uncle Barney, who will inherit the family empire, and no doubt run it to ruin.

Mockingly matched to the emblematic ravens whose gathering signals trouble in the Gursky saga are the "sodden partridges, drunk from pecking at fallen, fermented crab apples" that crash against Moses Berger's window as he pursues his lonely quest. Fraternally linked to the whiskey-soaked Moses as he crashes against the many obstacles that keep him from completing his task, the partridges can count on Moses's sympathy and help.

One of them wakened Moses with a start, slamming into his window and sliding to the grass. Responding to the brotherly call of another dipso in trouble, Moses yanked on his trousers and hurried outside. (9)

The huge black raven on the dust cover of *Solomon Gursky Was Here* and also on the frontispiece to the book is associated not only with Moses Berger but also with Mordecai Richler, author of the book. A voracious scavenger, the raven is not a pretty bird. In Innuit lore, it is known as "Raven" spelled with a capital "R." Raven is a trickster who likes to meddle in people's affairs and provoke trouble. As both Raven and raven, Richler is a voracious scavenger—of books and lives, including his own—which he satirizes and parodies. He meddles in people's affairs by fictionalizing them in his novels, and he stirs up plenty of trouble, exemplified by the commotion he caused by writing this book.

Not only has Richler been accused of profound disrespect toward the Bronfman family, but also of blackening the reputation of A.M. Klein—a much admired Montreal Jewish poet—who seems to be the model for Moses Berger's unscrupulous father in the book. The father, called L.B. Berger, is depicted as a highly regarded Montreal Jewish poet who "sells out" to become Bernard Gursky's speechwriter. He also tries to ruin his own son's promising writing career. While A.M. Klein did become a speechwriter to the liquor baron, Sam Bronfman, the failed relationship between Moses and his father, L.B. Berger, is pure fiction. It supplies the springboard for Moses to seek out a surrogate father, and ultimately propels Moses into writing his book.

However, years before he tries to sabotage his son's writing career, L.B. Berger introduces Moses to the Gursky family—thereby giving him a subject worthy of his talent and a mentor who will guide and inspire him. Solomon Gursky, working in mysterious ways, makes sure that Moses stumbles on memoirs, maps and notebooks that give him a detailed knowledge of the Gursky family history. But the main current that flows beneath this story of the Gurskys' booze-blessed wealth, is the primal longing of a son for his father's love, and a father's yearning for a son who will be worthy to carry forward all that is best in the family heritage. As Ephraim chooses his grandson Solomon, teaching him to survive the dangers of the far north and the devious cruelty of his older brother, so Solomon reaches outside the Gursky family to adopt Moses as true singer of the family songs.

The songs that Ephraim teaches Solomon who passes them on to Moses include the story of Aaron, Ephraim's only legitimate son, whom he fathered in an absent-minded moment in a quickly forgotten marriage on a brief trip to the old country. Aaron and his sons, however, become part of the dizzying challenge and elation that went with opening up Canada's western frontier where Bernard, Solomon, and Morrie, the rum-running, bootlegging, hotel-buying Gursky descendents of Ephraim begin to make their fortune. In his telling of the Gurskys' early days, Moses includes the happy days of his own childhood when he loved and looked up to his father and the literary circle of his father's friends, who made Moses as a young boy feel cherished and safe.

In all his singing of songs and telling of tales, Moses imitates his author, Mordecai Richler, who fictionalizes and parodies the Bronfman family history, the early explorers of the far North, the opening of the far West and the history of the liquor trade in Canada. Within the novel, Moses Berger (like his creator) tilts at windmills; fights for a truth and justice obscured by the deceptive surface of things; and searches for the real story behind the glittering facade of Gursky wealth and privilege. *Solomon Gursky Was Here* is a massive book—part biography (auto and otherwise), part rollicking adventure story, part biblical parody, part prophecy, and all Richler at the peak of his wicked wit.

Barney's Version: Summing Up

Late in spring Herzog had been overcome by the need to explain, to have it out, to justify, to put in perspective, to clarify, to make amends....
Considering his entire life, he realized that he had mismanaged everything—everything. (Herzog, 2,3)

Taking his cue from Saul Bellow's novel *Herzog*—written when Bellow was in his late forties and had recently undergone a messy divorce—Richler in his mid-sixties, married to a loving wife but no longer in good health, tackles Bellow's theme of a hopelessly mismanaged existence with boisterous zeal. *Herzog* is not really the story of a man who has bungled every aspect of his life and is now seeking to make amends. It is rather a betrayed man's attempt to understand what brought him to his present wretched state. Herzog's wife Madeleine had first persuaded him to give up his university job and buy a house in the country. Then she convinced him to move back to the city and fix up another house with expensive furniture. Finally she implored him to find a job in the same city for Valentine Gersbach, a close family friend who (unbeknownst to Herzog) was Madeleine's lover.

When she was well settled she demanded that Herzog leave their new house and give her a divorce, with custody of their child, on the grounds that their marriage no longer worked. Herzog, for a long time not realizing that Valentine was Madeleine's lover, confided in the man he thought was his friend. Valentine called Madeleine a "poor crazy bitch" but advised Herzog to give her what she wanted. Later, when Herzog found out that Valentine had been part of Madeleine's scheme all along, he completely fell apart.

At one point he even took his father's old gun, determined to kill the two people who had robbed and hoodwinked him. But when—looking through the window of his former house—he saw Valentine tenderly bathing their child, he knew he couldn't do it and went away. A day later with the gun still in his pocket, he became involved in a minor car accident. When the police discovered he was carrying a gun without a permit they took him to jail. Since Saul Bellow actually lived through this whole embarrassing sequence of events, the novel *Herzog* is to a large extent his own story in the guise of fiction.

When Richler writes *Barney's Version* he adopts Bellow's tactics. But Richler's "own story" is infiltrated with Bellow's "own story;" and both are woven into a narrative line that is pure invention. Barney calls the result of all this interweaving "the true story of my wasted life"—Barney's, not Richler's—even though large chunks of Richler's life may be found in it. Indeed part of the pleasure in reading this novel lies in recognizing where Barney ends and Richler begins.

Writing a parody of Bellow's story about a good man being duped by a sexy, lying, crazy bitch who likes to shop, has expensive tastes, and eventually goes off with another man, Richler immediately divides Herzog's wife Madeleine into three wives—otherwise known as "Barney's Troika." The first wife Clara is manipulative, promiscuous, artistic, and crazy. She eventually kills herself, which burdens Barney with guilt for the rest of his life. The second wife, who is known only as the second Mrs. Panofsky" (a salute to Herzog's Madeleine, mostly called "the second Mrs. Herzog"), loves to shop in expensive stores. She ends up in the bed of Barney's best friend "Boogie," which enables Barney to divorce her and marry his one true love, Miriam. Barney's third wife—whom he meets and falls in love with at his wedding to the second Mrs. Panofsky—is everything he ever wanted and more than he could ever expect. But Barney, through a hopeless blunder, manages eventually to drive her away.

Since the three sections into which Richler divides his novel are named after Barney's three wives, it would seem that the women in Barney's Troika hold the key to this massive multi-layered book. We will therefore (regretfully) put to one side the part of *Barney's Version* that relates to his work as the producer of "Totally Unnecessary Productions." We will put to another side the endearingly conflicted relationships he has with his children, colleagues and friends. This will enable us to grasp the key his three wives hold to the center of Barney's being; and to distinguish fiction from fact in Richler's outrageous fictionalizing of his life.

The most purely imaginative part of the story is the plot—originating in Saul Bellow's *Herzog*—and carried to wondrous heights. The *Herzog* part of the plot begins with the second Mrs. Panofsky's infidelity with Barney's best friend. It veers off from *Herzog* when Barney threatens the friend with a pistol left in the house by Barney's father, a retired cop. It ascends to vertiginous heights when friend "Boogie" unaccountably but completely disappears; Barney is accused of his murder; but is saved from a very long prison sentence by the intercession of a chubby Catholic priest. Even so, Barney is branded as a murderer well into his own demented old age: only to be vindicated at last by an airplane that flies directly out of Bellow's book.

The scandal surrounding the disappearance of Boogie—Barney's friend and mentor—is a red herring from the start, or rather a narrative hook that is only released in the last few lines. But it creates a thread of tension in the novel that ties it to *Herzog's* non-smoking gun and the sudden intrusion of a noisy plane. The episode provides a magnificent example of the way Richler can take a line from another writer's work, and put his own spin on it.

In Bellow's novel, "a jet plane—something screaming with great power at a terrible height—" awakens Herzog after a night of love with the woman who will probably become his third wife. This noisy airplane appears to signal a change for the better in Herzog's life.

In *Barney's Version*, Barney has fallen into a drunken sleep after threatening Boogie with his father's pistol and firing a shot over his head as drug-befuddled Boogie goes for a swim in the lake. Suddenly "A roaring, like an airplane engine, shook the room, and I dreamt that my plane was going down." This intrusive airplane means little to the reader at the time; neither do we see any connection later when we learn that Boogie's bones have been found on the top of a nearby mountain. Only in the "Afterword" to the novel, written by Barney's son Michael, do we learn how and why Boogie disappeared. As Michael speaks we finally connect the dots.

> *I was sitting on the porch...remembering old times, when suddenly a big fat water bomber came roaring in. It lowered onto the lake and, without even stopping, scooped up who knows how many tons of water, flew off, and dumped the water on the mountain....Benoit O'Neil explained that it was a practice run by forest-fire fighters in training. Years ago, he said, they used to fly over more often.* (417)

Aha! An amazing but plausible solution to the mystery of Barney's alleged crime: "the big fat water bomber" is the last piece of the puzzle. Obviously a similar water plane had scooped up Boogie's drowned body and dumped it on the top of Mont Groulx where it was subsequently ravaged by animals (who destroyed any evidence of whether Boogie had or had not been shot). The water plane becomes a *deus ex machina,* first hiding and then revealing the secret to Boogie's disappearance; first implicating Barney and then exonerating him from any crime. Sadly, Barney by this time is so far gone that he is beyond understanding what his son has figured out.

Three events are taken directly from Saul Bellow's *Herzog*: Boogie's betrayal of his friend by bedding his wife; Barney's threat to kill him with his father's gun; and Barney's involvement with the police. But Richler complicates the story with Boogie's sudden, mysterious disappearance, and then his equally puzzling reappearance as a pile of bones on a mountain. Since in Montreal there is a cemetery on top of Mount Royal, the friend's being reduced to a pile of bones on a mountain refers back to Richler's dedication at the beginning of his book: "In memory of four absent friends." At this point the name "Boogie," or as Barney tenderly calls him "the Boogie Man," tells us that he represents the loss of not just one friend but all those friends who are lost and gone. Indeed, loss maintains a constant presence in this otherwise upbeat novel; and Barney's frequent memory fade-outs keep us aware of this even while we laugh at Richler's humor.

Barney gives a plausible explanation for his frenzy of explaining, justifying, putting into perspective, clarifying, and attempting to make amends. But a deeper reason is that he is trying to hold on to happier times in the past and to absent friends, as his memory becomes less and less reliable.

> *Terry's the spur. The splinter under my fingernail. To come clean, I'm starting on this shambles that is the true story of my wasted life…as a riposte to the scurrilous charges Terry McIver has made in his forthcoming autobiography: about me, my three wives…the nature of my friendship with Boogie, and, of course, the scandal I will carry to my grave like a humpback.* (1)

Barney's version of why he is writing his memoirs is that "Terry McIver"—a writer he was never quite friendly with in Paris when they were young, or in Montreal when they were growing old—is writing a book that will show Barney in a very bad light. Therefore Barney must write his own version of events to set the record straight. Here Barney is speaking for Richler, giving us one of Richler's reasons for writing *Barney's Version*. Richler had recently given Michael Coren—abrasive host of the Michael Coren Show on CFRB and biographer of G.K. Chesterton, H.G. Wells, Arthur Conan Doyle, and C.S. Lewis—permission to be his official biographer. He must have realized not long after that he had lost control of the way his life would be presented; and therefore decided to get his own highly fictionalized *Version* out first. Later, when Michael Coren withdrew from the project, "Terry McIver" of whose version Barney has been so afraid, suddenly dies in the book.

Of Barney's three wives, the second Mrs. Panofsky—by sleeping with Barney's most esteemed friend—serves mainly as Richler's link to Bellow's novel. But unlike the situation in *Herzog* where Madeleine's husband is devastated by the betrayal, Barney is overjoyed when he realizes that he now has a good excuse to divorce the wife he should never have married, and marry the woman he really loves. Richler's cynical twist on his borrowing from Bellow is pure parody: linking *Barney's Version* to *Herzog* and establishing critical distance at the same time. It also refers to Richler's state of mind when his first wife betrayed him, giving him cause to leave her and marry his beloved Florence.

Richler's novels from first to last parody themes, characters, and incidents from books by writers he admires, and Saul Bellow ranks high among his favorites. However Richler's way of showing this admiration is always to alter what he has borrowed so that it reflects his own wit, his own circumstances, and his own way of looking at the world. A classic case of betrayal by one's wife and best friend becomes an occasion for joy and relief.

A darker shadow hovers over the way that Richler portrays Barney's first wife Clara—whom Barney marries out of pity and because she convinces him that she is carrying his child. She turns out to be a talented, manipulative, promiscuous neurotic who sleeps with Barney's friends even while denying Barney the dubious pleasure of her body. When she miscarries and her child turns out to have dark skin, Barney accosts Cedric, a good-looking black friend of his with whom Clara had been especially friendly.

> "I honestly don't know what to do now, Cedric, maybe I should hit you."
> "Goddamn it, Barney, I hate to tell you this, but I wasn't the only one."
> "Oh."
> "Didn't you know that much?"
> "No."
> "She's insatiable."

> *"Not with me she isn't."*
> *"Okey. Now listen to your Uncle Remus. You're only twenty three years old and she's a nut case. Shake her loose. Divorce her."* (120)

Although Cathy—Richler's first wife whom he married when he was twenty-three (against his better judgment and against the advice of those who knew him best)—was not a promiscuous, talented, manipulative nut case, she apparently did sleep with some of Richler's friends and she did convince him to marry her when he did not want to. From Michael Posner's book *The Last Honest Man* we also learn that Cathy and the fictional Clara shared certain physical characteristics: Cathy is described as "very tall and very very thin, taller than Mordecai, very angular, with flashing black eyes—like a character in one of his last books" (*The Last Honest Man*, 93-94).

> *It would be inaccurate to describe Clara as tall. Long is what she was. Skinny enough for a rib count. Her hands constantly in movement, adjusting her shawls, smoothing her skirts, brushing back her hair, peeling labels off bottles. Her fingers were nicotine and ink-stained, her nails were broken or bitten to the quick. Ears the shape of teacup handles protruding from her hair…that cascaded to her narrow waist. She had only the faintest of eyebrows, her huge black eyes lit with intelligence. And scorn. And panic.* (*Barney's Version*, 57)

According to Posner's book, Richler was worried that Cathy might become pregnant, because if they had a child he would have to stay in the marriage. And Cathy did become pregnant but miscarried, which Richler reported to William Weintraub with a certain amount of humor. In *Barney's Version* everything that relates Clara to Cathy is grotesquely exaggerated: her personality, her promiscuity, the circumstances of her marrying Barney, and the way she reacts after Barney leaves. Clara commits suicide while—according to *The Last Honest Man*—Cathy only had a nervous breakdown.

The way Richler fictionalizes the true story of his life with Florence is very different from his reconfiguration of the relationship with Cathy. And even when he is being humorous, the deep, clear love shines through. Barney's first sight of Miriam at his wedding to the second Mrs. Panofsky is only one day removed from Richler's actual meeting and falling in love with Florence, the day before his and Cathy's actual wedding.

Barney tells it this way:

> *Immediately we were pronounced man and wife, I kissed the bride, and made straight for the bar....*
> *Ill at ease among so many strangers at the Ritz, my mood unspeakable until everything changed. Then and forever. Across the crowded room...there stood the most enchanting woman I had ever seen. Long hair black as a raven's wing, striking blue eyes, ivory skin, slender, wearing a layered blue chiffon cocktail dress, and moving about with the most astonishing grace. Oh, that face of incomparable beauty. Those bare shoulders. My heart ached at the sight of her.*
> (206-7)

Richler's first meeting with Florence took place less heart-stoppingly at a friend's flat, and it was at their second meeting a day later at his own wedding reception that he followed her to the bar and made clear his great interest. After that the newly wed Richlers and the already married Florence and Stanley Mann became good friends. The two couples remained friends, to the point of deciding a few years later to share a villa in Roquebrune (near Monte Carlo). And there the story took a dramatic turn—either for better or for worse, depending on who is telling the story. According to Florence things worked out very well; according to Cathy it was a disaster. At some point during that chummy summer Richler told Cathy he didn't love her anymore and he wanted a divorce, after which Cathy left the villa. Florence and Stanley's marriage had been faltering for some time because of Stanley's philandering (according to *The Last Honest Man*), and the holiday with the Richlers had been an attempt at reconciliation. Because of the burgeoning romance between Florence and Richler, the Manns' marriage was clearly doomed, and Stanley left the villa as well.

In *Barney's Version* Richler replays his courtship of Florence and the winning of her love: only the situation is played in reverse. After Barney manages to divorce the second Mrs. Panofsky and marry Miriam, they live happily together for many years, raising their family and watching the children flourish. But Barney has grown complacent and no longer makes Miriam feel loved and wanted (a reprise of the situation that Florence found herself in with Stanley Mann). And so a snake slides into Barney's Garden of Eden, destroying his happiness forever.

> *Blair Hopper ne Hauptman had entered my life like an unwanted polyp in the summer of 1969. He had turned up at our cottage in the Laurentians (where Miriam, that bleeding heart welcomed troubled kids, abused wives, and other flotsam) on a rainy evening, having found our address in the <u>Manual for Draft-Age Immigrants to Canada.</u>* (316.)

> *Blair was contaminating my Yasnaya Polyana. Our ten lakeside acres. After crazy Clara, following the crap I went through with the second Mrs. Panofsky, my trial and subsequent disgrace, the dipshit TV business I hated but that continued to earn me big bucks. Miriam was my winning ticket. My redeemer....But my epiphany was tainted by fear. Surely the gods on Olympus had taken down my number for remedial action.*
> *—Get Panofsky. Crash his next Air Canada flight.*
> *—Hmmm.*
> *—Or what would you say to testicular cancer. Snip, snip. Off with his balls.* (321)

Although Blair has fallen in love with Miriam and Barney is getting nervous, there is no serious danger until Barney stumbles, making the fatal error that will drive his love away. He has a foolish, drunken one-night stand while Miriam is briefly out of town, forgetting that infidelity was the one thing that Miriam could not forgive. Her enjoyment of Blair's devotion at a time when Barney no longer made her feel special was innocent; but when Barney betrayed her trust she removed herself from his life. In real life, it was Stanley's behavior with other women that undermined his marriage to Florence; and when Richler threw himself at her feet, she threw Stanley out.

However when Barney in the novel compares Blair's arrival at his house to "an unwanted polyp" entering his life, a dark resonance sounds between fiction and fact. Richler had a cancerous polyp removed in 1993. Five years later he was operated on for cancer of the kidney. Three years after that the cancer took his life.

The basic plot of *Barney's Version* is pure fiction. Barney clearly knows that he is to blame for Miriam's going off with Blair. He also knows that he is blameless in the disappearance of his friend. It is not the death of Boogie but the death of his marriage that leaves him alone, unhappy and afraid. He painfully remembers and painstakingly sets down everything he has done wrong, hoping he can still make things right before his fading memory obliterates everything.

In his parody of Herzog's shambled existence, Richler creates an aging Barney who has neither wife nor life's work to give him comfort. While Herzog in Bellow's novel is a professor and writer—albeit during most of the novel unable to work—Barney is titular head of a film production company called "Totally Unnecessary Productions" to which he himself has now become totally unnecessary. Neither does Barney have a foreseeable future. Herzog, at the time of his imploded marriage, was in his forties and soon was on the way to marriage number three. At the end of the book he was beginning to resume his professional life. Barney is in his sixties, his marriage and occupation at an end, sliding ever more quickly into Alzheimer's disease. Yet the story Bellow tells is filled with rue, while Richler's *Version* (along with the pain and loss) is full of irrepressible, hilarious life.

Having thoroughly confused any future biographer by mixing aspects of his own life (such as his age, happy years with Florence and their children, and fierce loyalty to friends) with plot elements from *Herzog* and liberal streaks of pure inventiveness, Richler tells Barney's story in several voices. Barney pours out his heart in a richly humorous, grandly Jewish style, while Terry McIver—the so-called biographer whose slander Barney fears—displays a humorless pedantry. Barney's son Michael, to whom he entrusts the completion of his Memoirs, and who inserts footnotes where he believes his father has erred in places, names, and dates, speaks with a cool, English accent, sounding very young. From time to time, the second Mrs. Panofsky does her spoiled Jewish Princess comic turn, endearing herself to the reader even while she thoroughly antagonizes her hapless husband, who cannot understand why he ever married her.

The much-feared future biographer, Terry McIver, dies part way through *Barney's Version*. But Terry leaves behind the poignant title of his proposed biography, *Time and Fevers* (taken from W.H. Auden's poem, "Lay your sleeping head, my love"):

> *Time and fevers burn away*
> *Individual beauty from*
> *Thoughtful children, and the grave*
> *Proves the child ephemeral.*

Richler particularly admired this poem, which he had earlier used as epigraph to *Joshua Then and Now*. Its reprise in *Barney* refers not just to the darker theme of age being associated with loss, but also reminds us that Richler is writing not only Barney's life story, but a fictionalized version of his own as well. By the end of the novel, time and fevers had reduced Barney to a child-like shell, and in the "Afterword" it is Barney's son who finishes the story and solves the mystery that shadowed his father's life. After Richler's death, only four years after *Barney's Version* is published, his children write their versions of his life story, leaving many of his mysteries intact.

Barney's Version (published in 1997) introduces characters about whom we have mixed feelings, since they have the same names as individuals found in Richler's previous novels. The name "Barney," although explained in his *Version* as coming from a comic strip, had already been used in *The Acrobats,* Richler's first published novel, where it belonged to Barney Larkin, an unhappy middle-aged American with a flagrantly unfaithful wife. Coupling the name "Barney" with the surname "Panofsky" recalls the genial Communist Mr. Panofsky in *Son of a Smaller Hero,* and the crazy pseudo-scientist Panofsky in *The Incomparable Atuk.* Richler thereby adds undertones to the Barney Panofsky character that go beyond what Barney tells us about himself. If we take his past incarnations into account, we understand more fully that he has indeed a great deal to "explain, justify, clarify, and put into perspective."

The name of Barney Panofsky's cherished wife, his "heart's desire," Miriam, now married to someone else, recalls another name out of Richler's past novels. In *Son of a Smaller Hero,* Miriam is the wife of Noah Adler's English professor, who befriends Noah and invites Noah to come and live with him and his wife. Noah falls in love with Miriam and steals her from her husband. A few months later, he realizes that he no longer loves her and essentially gives her back. Toward the end of that novel, Noah hopes to "someday [be] a wiser Noah [living] in another cottage near a stream with a less neurotic Miriam."(*Son of a Smaller Hero,* 229)

In *Barney's Version,* Barney has found his heart's desire, that "less-neurotic Miriam" with whom he lives in a cottage near a lake. But he loses her in an ironic reversal of the earlier story. In Richler's final novel, a handsome young draft dodger, Blair Hopper, comes to Canada and, for a time, lives with Barney and Miriam. He falls in love with Miriam and becomes her trusted friend. Some time passes and Blair moves from Montreal to Toronto; Barney's behavior as a husband deteriorates to the point that he eventually commits his foolish drunken infidelity; Miriam leaves him and she marries Blair. Until his mind is so clouded by Alzheimer's that he believes Miriam has never left, Barney clings to the hope that Miriam will change her mind and one day return.

While Miriam is Barney's one good wife whom he loses through sheer inattention and stupidity, his first marriage is a disaster reminiscent of the situation in his third novel, *A Choice of Enemies,* where Norman Price marries a woman he doesn't even like. Barney makes the mistake of marrying a woman he doesn't like—twice.

Clara's dark-skinned miscarried child reminds us of Seymour Bone's wife in *The Incomparable Atuk,* who tells her husband not to be surprised if their baby turns out to be sort of "chocolaty." Clara's staged suicide, that leads to her death because her estranged husband doesn't come home, recalls the attention-seeking suicide that unintentionally succeeds in *A Choice of Enemies*. These events, played out again in Barney—the unborn child that is not the husband's and the staged suicide that goes badly wrong—are related to fears that did not materialize in Richler's early life, but nevertheless left behind a guilt that endured.

Barney's poor choice in his first two wives is equaled by his misplaced admiration for the friend he affectionately calls "the Boogieman." Barney looks up to Boogie as a writing genius, mentor, and guide through life, although Boogie never finished his first, long promised novel and his life is a drug distorted mess. As a deeply flawed mentor, constantly on the move, serving as moral editor even though he has no morals of his own, Boogie resembles the dark side of Joey Hersh, the Horseman in Richler's seventh novel *St. Urbain's Horseman.* In everyday life a swindler, bigamist, and tax-evader, the Horseman became Jake's hero and guide because he had a wild heart, had fought in the Spanish Civil War and was thought to be tracking down Nazi criminals in the wilds of South America. Whether he was as courageous as Jake believed, or whether he was the fraud the rest of the family maintained, he gave Jake something larger than his own life to aspire to.

Boogie is a small, sick version of the shining Horseman: a false moral guide who ends up as a pile of bones and is finally put to rest.

While Barney remembers his misspent existence, trying to make sense of the things he has thought and done, Richler keeps reaching back into his earlier books, reevaluating people, places, ideas, and events. *The Apprenticeship of Duddy Kravitz* presents us with Richler's most memorable character until Barney comes along, and Duddy bequeathes to Barney his money making skills (at times legitimate, but more often not). When a mature Duddy appears in *St. Urbain's Horeman,* he brings along a Jewish Princess wife who, together with Harvey Schwartz's wife Becky in *Solomon Gursky Was Here,* knows all there was to know about making a husband miserable. This type of woman is one that Richler thankfully never married, but he was able to observe her with a shudder among people he knew.

Florence, the woman who made Richler happy in real life, giving up her modeling career to be a great wife and mother, becomes the model for each of the husband-pleasing wives in his books. She first appears in a minor role as Hy Rosen's wife Diana in *Cocksure,* and returns as Nancy, Jake Hersh's wife in *St. Urbain's Horseman.* She is Pauline, Joshua's lost and found wife in *Joshua Then and Now,* and Diana Morgan, loved and lost by Solomon in *Solomon Gursky Was Here.* She ends up as Barney's third wife, Miriam, and is lost again.

The Incomparable Atuk is truly incomparable in that the Florence character is actually an undercover Royal Canadian Mounted Policeman in drag who falls in love with the Richler-in-drag character, Jean-Paul McEwan. At the end of *The Incomparable Atuk* the Royal Canadian Mounted Policeman, code named Jane, is on his/her way to winning a Miss Universe contest.

While Richler lovingly parodies his beloved second wife, his parody is intense and cruel when it comes to the woman he married first, and it is filled with ambivalence regarding women he was with before his first marriage. In his three earliest novels, Richler pairs the main character (who invariably parallels Richler at the time) with young women who induce a sense of inadequacy and guilt. Andre's first girlfriend dies during her abortion of his baby in *The Acrobats*, for which Andre never forgives himself. The first Miriam, Noah's girl friend in *Son of a Smaller Hero*, is an unhappy, unfulfilled wife who becomes neurotically dependent on Noah during the brief time she is with him, and turns into a promiscuous drunk when he cuts himself loose. Written while Richler was married to Cathy, the fate of this first Miriam mirrors Richler's fears of what might happen to Cathy if he leaves her. *A Choice of Enemies* ends with Norman marrying a woman who has been briefly kind to him but is otherwise malicious and self involved. Their marriage, doomed from the start, also reflects the unhappiness of Richler's first plunge into matrimonial waters, although, according to Richler's friends, Cathy was not like either of the women in his second or third novels.

"Who is it that can tell me who I am?" asks Shakespeare's King Lear as his mind spirals out of control. How can I make sense out of my mismanaged life? asks Barney Panofsky as his memory clouds and fades. Along with everything else that Barney represents, he is also Richler's King Lear: struggling with old age, loss, loneliness, and regret. As Lear, out of pride and arrogance, sends away his loving daughter Cordelia, so Barney, out of thoughtless stupidity, sends his loving Miriam into another man's arms. And as, for a short period, Lear is reunited with Cordelia; so, when Barney's mind is almost obliterated by dementia, Miriam briefly returns to him, not as his wife but as a compassionate friend. Fortunately, Barney has deteriorated to such an extent that he cannot tell the difference.

Barney's Version like Richler's other novels parodies great works of literature that have gone before. At the same time it chronicles in a self-mocking way the changes in Richler's life as he goes from age to age. Therefore in true Richler style the tragedy of Barney and his three wives comes wrapped in layers of comic invective. But underneath the humor and the brilliant set pieces; under the political diatribes and the reappearance of characters from earlier novels; the narrative hook of whether or not Barney murdered his best friend; is a theme as tragic, powerful, and human as Shakespeare's *King Lear*. While Richler's borrowings from Saul Bellow's *Herzog* drive the plot, it is Barney's incarnation as a modern King Lear—"a foolish, fond old man" who has lost...everything—that wrenches the heart.

Afterword

We shall not cease from exploration
And the end of all our exploring
Will be to arrive where we started
And know the place for the first time.
(T.S. Eliot, *Four Quartets*)

Like T.S. Eliot who deepens the meaning of his poems by bringing in echoes from religion, myth, legend, and drama, Mordecai Richler thickens the texture of his novels by weaving in ancient and contemporary literary strands, including some from Eliot's poems. Although Eliot from time to time also writes parody, Richler's parody is so thoroughgoing that it becomes his defining method and distinguishing technique. In every novel he subtly or overtly distances himself from the sources he depends on.

I wrote *Mordecai Richler: A Life in Ten Novels* as a tribute to Richler, and as a way of sharing my fascination with the way he combines a fictional version of his life with parodies of his literary sources. Richler's use of parody is an astonishing, generally underrated, achievement. Like Shakespeare, he takes well known characters, plots, and ideas from writers he admires, and inserts them into his own highly individual literary works, stirring up undercurrents of meaning to deepen and expand on both the borrowed stories and the ones he creates.

When he uses biblical names for his characters, he ties their destinies to those of their biblical counterparts. Indeed, so pervasive is the Bible in Richler's novels, and so memorable are the characters in his books, that his novels tend to complicate our attitude toward the Bible stories he had the audacity to parody. Similarly, when we go back and read any of the novels or poems that he wove into his novels, our reaction to the original will evermore remind us of his ingenious reworking.

Because his novels provide such a rich feast, and yield new delights each time we read them, and because they are so firmly entrenched in some of the best of our literary tradition, Richler's place in the literary pantheon is secure. And for those of us who grew up and grew old along with him as he fictionalized his own life in the lives of his characters, his place in our hearts is secure as well.

Bibliography

Richler's Novels

Richler, Mordecai. *The Acrobats.* London: Andre Deutsch, 1954.

———. *Son of a Smaller Hero.* London: Andre Deutsch, 1955.

———. *A Choice of Enemies.* London: Andre Deutsch, 1957.

———. *The Apprenticeship of Duddy Kravitz.* London: Andre Deutsch, 1959.

———. *The Incomparable Atuk.* Toronto: McClelland and Stewart, 1963.

———. *Cocksure.* New York: Simon and Schuster, 1968.

———. *St. Urbain's Horseman.* Toronto: McClelland and Stewart, 1971.

———. *Joshua Then and Now.* Toronto: McClelland and Stewart, 1980.

———. *Solomon Gursky Was Here.* Markham, Ontario: Viking, Penguin Books, 1989.

———. *Barney's Version.* Toronto: Alfred A. Knopf, 1997.

Other Writings

Richler, Mordecai. "We Jews Are Almost As Bad As Gentiles." *Maclean's,* October 22, 1960.

———. *Hunting Tigers Under Glass: Essays and Reports.* Toronto: *Maclean's,* October 22, 1960.

_____. *The Street.* Toronto: McClelland and Stewart, 1969; rpt. Penguin Books, 1977.

_____. *Shoveling Trouble.* Toronto: McClelland and Stewart, 1972.

_____. *Notes on an Endangered Species and Others.* New York: Knopf, 1974.

_____. *Home Sweet Home.* Toronto: McClelland and Stewart, 1984; rpt. Penguin Books, 1985.

_____. *Oh Canada! Oh Quebec!: Requiem for a Divided Country.* Toronto: Penguin Books, 1992.

_____. *Belling the Cat: Essays, Reports, and Opinions.* Canada: Alfred A. Knopf, 1998.

_____. "How I became an unknown with my first novel." (1958); rpt. *Maclean's,* July 16, 2001.

_____. Collected Papers. [Letters, Reviews, Working Notes, Research] University of Calgary Library, Special Collections.

Literary Criticism

Brenner, Rachel Feldhay. *Assimilation and Assertion: The Response to the Holocaust in Mordecai Richler's Writing.* New York: Peter Lang, 1989.

Craniford, Ada. *Fiction and Fact in Mordecai Richler's Novels.* Lewiston, New York: Edwin Mellen Press, 1992.

Darling, Michael. "Mordecai Richler: An Annotated Bibliography." *The Annotated Bibliography of Canada's Major Writers*, Vol. 1, Robert Lecker and Jack David, Eds. Downsview, Ontario: ECW Press, 1979.

Darling, Michael, Ed. *Perspectives on Mordecai Richler*. Toronto: ECW Press, 1968.

Davidson, Arnold. *Mordecai Richler*. New York: Ungar Press, 1983.

Gibson, Graham. "Mordecai Richler." *Eleven Canadian Novelists*. Toronto: Anansi, 1973.

Greenstein, Michael. "Mordecai Richler and Canadian Jewish Humor." *Jewish Wry*. Bloomington: Indiana Press, 1987.

McSweeney, Kerry. "Mordecai Richler." *Canadian Writers and their Works*. Fiction Series, Vol. 6. Robert Lecker, Jack David, Ellen Quigley, eds. Toronto: ECW Press, 1985.

Pacey, Desmond. *Canadian Writing in Canada*. Toronto: Ryerson Press, 1961.

Pollock, Zailig. "Duddy Kravitz and Betrayal." *Perspectives on Mordecai Richler*. Toronto: ECW Press, 1968.

Posner, Michael. *The Last Honest Man: Mordecai Richler, An Oral Biography*. Toronto: McClelland and Stewart, 2004.

Ramraj, V.J. *Mordecai Richler*. Boston: Twayne Books, 1983.

Sheps, David. *Critical Views on Canadian Writers: Mordecai Richler*. Toronto: McGraw-Hill-Ryerson, 1971.

Yanofsky, Joel. *Mordecai and Me: An Appreciation of a Kind*. Calgary: Red Deer Press, 2003.

Woodcock, George. *Mordecai Richler. Canadian Writers*, No. 6. Toronto: McClelland and Stewart, 1971.

Literary Sources that Richler Parodies
(Not necessarily from the editions I use.)

In *The Acrobats*:

Auden, W.H. "O Who Can Ever Gaze His Fill!" (1936). *Selected Poems*. New York Vintage Books, 1979. (Richler would have used an early edition.)

Hemingway, Ernest. *For Whom the Bell Tolls*. (1940).

_____. *The Sun Also Rises* (1926). (I did not consult specific texts for these two books).

Holy Bible, Revised Standard Edition. Gospels of Matthew and John.

Lowry, Malcolm. *Under the Volcano* (1947). Rpt. Harmondsworth, England: Penguin Books, 1962.

Rilke, Rainer Maria. "Fifth Elegy" (1915). *Duino Elegies*. Tr. David Young. New York: Norton, 1978. (Richler would have used an earlier translation; however the introduction to the Norton edition specifically mentions Picasso's *Acrobats* as inspiration for the elegy.)

In *Son of a Smaller Hero:*

The Holy Scriptures, Masoretic Text. Genesis 6: 1-28. (Story of Noah and the Ark).

Dostoyevsky, Fyodor. *The Brothers Karamazov*. (1879-1880). (Publication date was checked in *The Reader's Encyclopedia*. William Rose Benet, Ed. New York: Thomas Y Crowell, 1948.)

In *A Choice of Enemies:*

Eliot, T.S. "The Love Song of J. Alfred Prufrock." (1917). *Selected Poems.* London: Faber and Faber, 1954.

Sophocles (495-406 B.C.). "Oedipus the King." *Seven Famous Greek Plays.* New York: Random House, 1938, 1950.

Wilde, Oscar. *The Picture of Dorian Gray.* (1891); *The Importance of Being Earnest.* (1895). Collected in *The Works of Oscar Wilde.* London: Collins, (undated).

In *The Apprenticeship of Duddy Kravitz:*

The Holy Scriptures, Masoretic Text. 1 Samuel 17: 31-49. (The story of David)

Schulberg, Budd. *What Makes Sammy Run?.* New York: Random House, 1941.

In *The Incomparable Atuk:*

Cohen, Nathan. "Heroes of the Richler View." *Tamarack Review.* No. 6, 1957.

Gilbert and Sullivan. *The Mikado* (1885). (I consulted a libretto.)

Mordecai Richler Papers. Special Collections, University of Calgary Library Archives. Letters from Nathan Cohen.

In *Cocksure:*

Orwell, George. *Nineteen Eighty Four.* Harmondsworth, England: Penguin Books, 1949.

Richler, Mordecai. "Mortimer Griffin, Shalinsky, and How They Settled the Jewish Question." *Tamarack Review*, No. 7, Spring 1958.

In *St. Urbain's Horseman:*

Auden, W.H. "September 1, 1939." *Selected Poems.* Toronto: Random House, 1979. (Richler would have used an early edition of the poem.)

Holy Scriptures. Masoretic Text. Genesis 27: 1-29.

Holy Bible. Revised Standard Edition. Revelation 20:11.

Appollodorus. Loeb Classical Library Tr. James G. Frazer. "Hercules."(Checked with internet)

Bullfinch's Mythology. "The Age of Fables: Hercules." (Checked with internet)

In *Joshua Then and Now:*

Auden, W.H. "Lay Your Sleeping Head My Love." (1937) *Selected Poems.* Toronto: Random House, 1979. (Richler would have used another edition.)

Holy Scriptures. Masoretic Text.

_____. Joshua.

_____. Esther.

_____. Job.

_____. Ten Commandments. Exodus 20: 1-17.

Laurence, Margaret. *The Diviners.* New York: Knopf, 1974.

In *Solomon Gursky Was Here:*

Beattie, Owen and John Geiger. *Frozen in Time: Unlocking the Secrets of the Franklin Expedition.* Saskatoon: Western Producer Prairie Books, 1988.

Caplan, Usher. *Like One that Dreamed: A Portrait of A.M. Klein.* Toronto: McGraw-Hill Ryerson, 1982.

Newman, Peter C. *Bronfman Dynasty: The Rothchilds of the New World.* Toronto: McClelland and Stewart, 1978.

Rosenberg, Leah. *The Errand Runner: Reflections of a Rabbi's Daughter.* Toronto: John Wiley and Sons, 1981.

Symons, A.J.A. *The Quest For Corvo: An Experiment in Biography.* Harmondsworth, England: Penguin Books, 1934.

Holy Scriptures. Masoretic Text. Ten Commandments. Exodus 20: 1-17.

_____. The Story of the Burning Bush. Exodus 3: 1-14.

In *Barney's Version:*

Bellow, Saul. *Herzog.* London: Penguin Books, 1964.

Shakespeare, William. *King Lear (1603-6).* Signet Classic. New York: New American Library, 1963.

Background for the Novels and Articles Written After Richler's Death

Adilman, Sid. "Richler recovering from double blow." *The Toronto Star,* June 23, 1998.

Bellow, Saul. *Herzog.* Intr. Malcolm Bradbury. London: Penguin Books, 1964. (This edition was read for its informative Introduction.)

Cernetig, Miro. "Lead Poisoning from tin cans killed explorers, scientists say." *The Globe and Mail,* February 1, 1990.

Dabby, Victor. "Computers create 'synthetic actors.'" *The Globe and Mail,* June 16, 1987.

Dube, Francine. "Death from cancer comes as a shock." *National Post,* July 4, 2001.

Egan, Susanna. *Patterns of Experience in Autobiography.* Chapel Hill: University of North Carolina Press, 1984.

Fraser, John. "*Maclean's* drew Mordecai like no one else." *National Post,* July 25, 2001.

Fulford, Robert. "Seventy years of glorious trouble." *National Post,* July 4, 2001.

Gottlieb, Robert. "The Man from St. Urbain Street." *Time,* July 16, 2001.

Hamilton, Graeme. "Richler family bids farewell to 'the scrappiest of statesmen.'" *National Post,* July 6, 2001.

Hutcheon, Linda. *A Theory of Parody.* New York: Methuen, 1985.

_____. *The Canadian Postmodern.* New York: Oxford University Press, 1998.

Johnson, William. "Oh, Mordecai. Oh, Quebec." *The Globe and Mail,* July 7, 2001.

_____. "Mordecai Remembered." *Maclean's,* June 24, 2002.

O'Reilly, Finbarr. "Richler 'stable' after surgery." *The Globe and Mail,* June 10, 1990.

McKay, John. "Richler lands Leacock prize." www.montrealgazette.com, 16 April 1998.

Myers, Sean. "Richler's first novel uncovered." *The Vancouver Sun*, September 30, 2002.

Richler, Emma. *Sister Crazy*. Toronto: Alfred A. Knopf, 2001.

Richler, Jacob. "Writer, father, and king of sang froid." *National Post*, July 7, 2001.

Richler, Noah. "I wanted to do good for Pa." *National Post*, July 4, 2001.

Rosenberg, Leah. *The Errand Runner: Reflections of a Rabbi's Daughter*. Toronto: John Wiley and Sons, 1981.

Spotlight. "Richler Biographer." *The Toronto Star*, May 24, 1995.

Stoffman, Judy. "Richler novel wins Giller Prize." *The Toronto Star*, November 5, 1997.

———. "Larger than death." *Toronto Star*, April 3, 2004.

Weintraub, William. *Getting Started: A Memoir of the 1950s*. Toronto: McClelland and Stewart, 2001.

Wilson, Jonathan. *Herzog: The Limits of Ideas*. Boston: Twayne, 1990.

Wong, Jan. "Mordecai Richler's Rules for Drinking and Thriving." *The Globe and Mail*, September 25, 1997.

Reviews of Richler's Novels

Amiel, Barbara. "Desperate encounters of middle age: *Joshua Then and Now*." *Maclean's*, June 9, 1980. 51.

Arnold, Janice. "Richler biography an intimate portrait of a complex man." *The Canadian Jewish News*, April 1, 2004. (Review of *The Last Honest Man* by Michael Posner).

Ashwell, Keith. "From a Sparse Heritage to Room at the Top." *The Edmonton Journal,* March 13, 1970. 71.

Baruch, Gershon. "Books in Review: *Son of a Smaller Hero.*" *The Bulletin,* November 1955, Mordecai Richler Papers, 36.22.6.

Baskin, Bernard. "New Richler novel inspired by Bronfman family." *The Canadian Jewish News,* 30 November 1989. 41.

Bermant, Chaim. "Riding High: *St. Urbain's Horseman."* Mordecai Richler Papers, 36.30.12. (Detached from *Jewish Quarterly,* undated. 46-49)

———. Book Reviews. "Dual-level drama: *St. Urbain's Horseman."* *Jewish Chronicle,* Sept 3, 1971. Mordecai Richler Papers, 36.31.1.

———. "Just for Laughs." *Jewish Chronicle* (London). 10 May 1968. Mordecai Richler Papers, 36.18.10. (Review of *Cocksure).*

Birbalsingh, Frank. "Mordecai Richler and the Jewish Canadian Novel." *Journal of Commonwealth Literature,* June 1972. 73-82.

Bissell, Claude. "Letters in Canada: 1954." *University of Toronto Quarterly,* 24 (April 1955) 262. (Review of *The Acrobats).*

———. "Letters in Canada: 1955." *University of Toronto Quarterly,* 25 (April 1956) 305. (Review of *Son of a Smaller Hero).*

———. "Letters in Canada: 1957." *University of Toronto Quarterly,* 27 (July 1958) 457. (Review of *A Choice of Enemies).*

Bissoondath, Neil. "Classic Mordecai." *The (Montreal) Gazette,* 18 November 1989. K-9.9. (Review of *Solomon Gursky Was Here).*

Blais, Clark. "Rich and Funny, it's Richler's Best book yet." *The (Montreal) Gazette,* 22 May 1971. 44. (Review of *St. Urbain's* Horseman).

Brandeis, Robert C. "Up From St. Urbain." *Jewish Di'Al-Og,* (Summer 1973) 46-47.

Brooks, Jeremy. "Recent Fiction: *The Incomparable Atuk.*" Mordecai Richler Papers, 36.20.1.

Bryden, Ronald. "Bedbugs*: The Incomparable Atuk.*" *New Statesman,* 18 October 1963.

Buitenhuis, Peter. "Novel Satirizes Toronto Customs." *The Globe and Mail,* 23 November 1963. Mordecai Richler Papers: 36.20.1.

Burgess, Anthony. "A Good Man Destroyed—Hilariously." *Life Magazine,* 15 March 1968. 8. (Review of *Cocksure*).

Callaghan, Barry. "Books." *The Toronto Telegram,* 16 March 1968. Mordecai Richler Papers, 36,18,9. (Review of *Cocksure*).

Cameron, Donald. "Expatriate's Dilemma." Mordecai Richler Papers: 36.18.9. (Review of *Cocksure*).

_____. "Aren't We All Made of Flesh?" *The Nation,* June 1971. 759-66. (Review of *St. Urbain's Horseman*).

_____. "The Professional Canadian." *Canadian Literature,* no. 50 (Autumn 1971) 103-104.

_____. "*St. Urbain's Horseman*" *Maclean's,* May 1971. 80.

_____. "Don Mordecai and the Hardhats." *The Canadian Forum,* March 1972. 29-32.

_____. "Mordecai Richler: The Reticent Moralist." *Conversations with Canadian Novelists* Part II, Toronto: Macmillan, 1973. 114-27.

Carrol, John. "On Richler and Ludwig." *Tamarack Review,* 19 (Autumn 1963) 98-102. (Review of *The Incomparable Atuk*).

Cohen, Derek. "Mordecai Then and Now." *Canadian Forum,* August 1980. 26-28.

Cohen, Nathan. "A Conversation with Mordecai Richler." *The Tamarack Review,* (Winter 1957). 6-23.

Cude, Wilfred. "One Man's Golem." *A Due Sense of Difference.* Boston: University Press of America, 1980.

_____"The Golem as Metaphor for Art: The Monster Takes Meaning in *St. Urbain's Horseman." Journal of Canadian Fiction,* 12 no. 2 (1977): 50-69.

Davies, R.R. "New Fiction: Many Cravings." *New Statesman,* 3 September 1971. 108. (Review of *St. Urbain's Horseman*).

Davis, L.J. "A Dickensian novel about being a grown-up." *The Washington Post,* "Book World," 20 June 1971. 1, 3. (Review of *St. Urbain's Horseman*).

Disher, Scott. "Richler's Paradise Lost." *Books in Canada,* November 1997. (Review of *Barney's Version*).

Edwards, Thomas R. "Mordecai Richler Then and Now." *The New York Times Book Review,* 27 June 1980. 11, 24.

Ferns, John. "Sympathy and Judgement in Mordecai Richler's *The Apprenticeship of Duddy Kravitz." Journal of Canadian Fiction,* Vol. 3 no. 1 (Winter 1974) 77-82.

Festival. October 1962. "The Incomparable Mordecai." Mordecai Richler's Papers, 36.20.1.

Freedman, Adele. "Richler's Satiric Eye." *The Globe and Mail,* 17 May 1980 (Review of *Joshua then and Now*).

French, William. "Mordecai Richler comes down from the mountain with a message—or 10." *The Globe and Mail*, 24 May 1980.(Review of *Joshua then and Now*).

Fulford, Robert. *Anthology*, 6 January 1959. Mordecai Richler Papers, *36.17.10. 1-9*. (Untitled essay on Richler discussing *The Acrobats, Son of a Smaller Hero,* and *A Choice of Enemies*).

_____. "Welcome Back to Richler, Already an Old Master." *The Montreal Gazette*, 28 May 1966. (Review of *Son of a Smaller Hero* reissued in paperback).

_____. "Canadian Sammy Glick." *Toronto Daily Star*, 15 October 1959. (Review of *The Apprenticeship of Duddy Kravitz*).

_____. "Mordecai Richler embraces Mr. Sam." *The Financial Times*, 15 January 1990. (Review of *Solomon Gursky Was Here*).

_____ "Books in Revue: All the Mordecais together at last." *Saturday Night*, 25-26. Mordecai Richler Papers, 36.30.12. (Review of *St. Urbain's Horseman*).

_____. "Disgusting, dirty, funny, distinguished." *Toronto Daily Star*, 3 March 1967. (Review of *Cocksure*).

Godfrey, David. "A Major Canadian Novel." *Books in Canada,* May 1971. (Review of *St. Urbain's Horseman*).

Gold, Joseph. "From Jericho to Montreal: Richler's Latest Homecoming." Fiddlehead, 128 (Winter 1981). (Review of *Joshua Then and Now*).

Goodman, Walter. "Mordecai Richler Then and Now." *The New York Times Book Review,* 22 June 1980.

Gordon, Sheldon. "Searching for Solomon." *The Financial Times*, 20 November 1989.

Greenstein, Michael. "The Apprenticeship of Noah Adler." *Canadian Literature,* 78 (Autumn 1978).

Harlow, Robert. "Telling it in Garth." *Books in Canada,* May 1980. (Review of *Joshua Then and Now*).

Harpur, Tom. "Richler: We have to be gentle with other people." *Toronto Star,* 23 October 1981. (Interview).

Hatch, Robert. "Man With a Marvy Lymph System." *The Nation,* 1 April 1968. Mordecai Richler Papers, 36.18.9. (Review of *Cocksure*).

Heichelman, F.M. "*Son of a Smaller Hero* has Valuable Lessons to Teach." *The Jewish Standard,* 15 November 1955. Mordecai Richler Papers, 36.22.6.

Honore, Carl. "Italians Make Folk Hero of Barney." *National Post,* "Arts and Life," July 4, 2001.

Hughes, Isabel. "Montreal's Richler Unhappy in London." *The Globe and Mail,* 30 November 1957. (Review of *A Choice of Enemies*).

Jackson, Marni. "A Poke in the I." *The Globe and Mail,* August 18, 2001. (Review of *Barney's Version*).

Jason, Philip K. "Types of the Jewish Hero: *St. Urbain's Horseman.*" *The Jewish Spectator,* October 1971.

Jeffrey, David L. "Artist as Middle-Aged Man." *Canadian Literature,* 88-91 (Summer 1981). (Review of *St. Urbain's Horseman*).

Jones, Mervyn. "Choose your enemies: *The Incomparable Atuk.*" *Tribune,* 22 November 1963.

Kardonne, Rick. "Richler's *Solomon Gursky Was Here* a disappointing bore." *The B'nai Brith Covenant,* November 1980.

Kattan, Naim. "Mordecai Richler: Craftsman or Artist." *Canadian Literature,* 21 (Summer 1964). Translated from the French by George Woodcock.

Knelman, Martin. "Ted Kotcheff: A wandering son heads for home to film Richler's Duddy Kravitz." *The Globe and Mail,* 19 August 1972.

Le Butt, Paul. "Book Column." *The Daily Gleaner,* March 30 (date incomplete) Mordecai Richler Papers, 36.18.9. (Review of *Cocksure*).

Lincoln, Richard. "A Hero with a marvy lymph system." *Book World,* 31 March 1968. Mordecai Richler Papers, 36.18.7. (Review of *Cocksure*).

Lyell, Frank H. "An Expatriate's Search for Truth." *New York Times and Book Review,* 2 January 1955. (Review of *The Acrobats*).

MacGregor, Roy. "The Boy From St. Urbain." *Maclean's,* 9 June 1980.

Mandel, E.W. "Two Novels: *The Apprenticeship of Duddy Kravitz.*" *Queen's Quarterly,* 67 (Spring 1960).

Matthews, Robin. "Messiah or Judas: Mordecai Richler Comes Home." *Canadian Review,* 1, no.1 (February 1974).

Metcalf, John. "Black Humor: An Interview with Mordecai Richler." *Journal of Canadian Fiction,* 3 no.1 (Winter 1974).

———. "New Novels." *Spectator,* 23 April 1954. (Review of *The Acrobats*).

Myers, David. "Mordecai Richler as Satirist." *Ariel,* 4 no. 1 (January 1973).

Ower, John. "Sociology, Psychology, and Satire in *The Apprenticeship of Duddy Kravitz.*" *Modern Fiction Studies,* 22 (1976).

Panofsky, Ruth. "A kinder, gentler Mordecai." *The Toronto Star,* September 27, 1997. (Review of *Barney's Version*).

Pollock, Zailig. "The Trial of Jake Hersh." *Journal of Canadian Fiction*, 22 (1978).

Prose, Francine. "Hopping Mad in Montreal." *The New York Times Book Review* 8 April 1990. (Review of *Solomon Gursky Was Here*).

Renzetti, Elizabeth. "The Public Face of Mordecai Richler." *The Globe and Mail*, September 27, 1997.

Ritts, Morton. "Witness to his time." *Maclean's*, 13 November 1989. (Review of *Solomon Gursky Was Here*).

Rooke, Leon. "Tales from the Caboose." *Books in Canada*, November 1989. (Review of *Solomon Gursky Was Here*).

Saunders, Tom. "Saga of an Unwilling Hero." *Winnipeg Free Press*, 6 April 1968. (Review of *Cocksure*).

Scott. Peter Dale. "A Choice of Certainties." *Tamarack Review*, 8 (1958). Rpt. *Critical Views on Canadian Writers*. Ed. G. David Sheps. Toronto: McGraw-Hill Ryerson. 1971.

Sheps, David. "Waiting for Joey: the Theme of the Vicarious in *St. Urbain's Horseman*." *Journal of Canadian Fiction*, 3 no. 1 (Winter 1974).

Siskind, Jacob. "Montrealer's Novel Not a Pleasant Tale." *The Montreal Star*, 1 October 1955. (Review of *Son of a Smaller Hero*).

Trevor, William. "Sex on its mind." *Guardian*, 19 April 1968. Mordecai Richler Papers, 36.19.9. (Review of *Cocksure*).

Wachtel, Eleanor. "Richler can't take his eyes off that familiar street." *The Vancouver Sun*, 6 June 1980. (Review of *Joshua then and Now*).

Walker, Joan. "Bitterly Dissatisfied." *The Globe and Mail*, 8 October 1955. (Review of *Son of a Smaller Hero*).

Warkentin, Germaine. "*Cocksure*: An Abandoned Introduction." *Journal of Canadian Fiction,* 4, no. 3. 1975.

Watmough, David. "Talking About Books." 8 November 1963. Mordecai Richler Papers, 36.20.2.

Watt, Frank. "Letters in Canada: 1963." *University of Toronto Quarterly,* 33 (July 1964). (Review of *The Incomparable Atuk*).

_____. "Auberon Waugh on Mr. Richler's jumbo sandwich." *Spectator,* 11 (September 1971). (Review of *St. Urbain's Horseman*).

Williamson, David. "Joshua: a Jew among Gentiles." *Winnipeg Free Press,* 31 May 1980.

Wisse, Ruth. "Books in Review: Debit in the Ledgers." *Congress Bulletin,* February 1960. (Review of *The Apprenticeship of Duddy Kravitz*).

Yardley, John. "*St. Urbain's Horseman.*" *New York Times Book Review,* 27 June (1971)

Index

A

A Choice of Enemies 5, 12, 39, 41, 46, 49, 68, 77, 80, 81, 82, 85, 134, 136, 141, 144, 150, 153, 154
A Theory of Parody xii, 28, 57, 148
Aaron 97, 111, 121
Abraham 119
Acrobats xi, 1, 2, 10, 19, 20, 21, 24, 25, 26, 27, 61, 64, 69, 107, 133, 136, 141, 143, 144, 150, 153, 155
Adilman, Sid 147
Amiel, Barbara 149
Andre Deutsch 10, 11, 12, 141
Appollodorus 146
Ark 3, 28, 29, 33, 34, 35, 38, 100, 144
Arnold, Janice 149
Ashwell, Keith 149
Assimilation and Assertion 142
Auden, W.H. 144, 146
Augean Stables 89, 91

B

Bar Mitzvah 9, 102
Baruch, Gershon 150
Baskin, Bernard 150
Belling the Cat 142
Bellow, Saul 147
Bermant, Chaim 150
Bible xii, 3, 4, 6, 7, 16, 28, 30, 34, 35, 37, 38, 53, 55, 57, 73, 88, 100, 102, 104, 105, 106, 109, 111, 112, 119, 139, 144, 146
Bissell, Claude 150
Bissoondath, Neil 150

Blessing 6, 36, 88, 112
Book of Esther 102, 103
Book of Joshua 102, 106
Books in Canada 152, 153, 156
Books in Review 150, 157
Boy Wonder 52, 53
Brandeis, Robert C. 150
Brooks, Jeremy 151
Brunhilde 74
Buitenhuis, Peter 151
Bulletin 150, 157
Bullfinch's Mythology 146
Burgess, Anthony 151

C

Callaghan, Barry 151
Cameron, Donald 151
Canadian Forum 151
Canadian Jewish News 149, 150
Canadian Literature 18, 53, 151, 153, 154
Canadian Writers and their Works 143
Caplan, Usher 147
Celine 1
Chaim 20, 23, 24, 150
Chosen Pagans 13, 75
Christ 2, 20, 21, 27
Christian 14, 33, 35, 74, 75, 79, 80, 84, 85, 90, 95
Cocksure 6, 14, 76, 77, 79, 80, 81, 82, 83, 84, 85, 86, 87, 88, 135, 141, 145, 150, 151, 153, 154, 155, 156
Cohen, Derek 151
Cohen, Nathan 145, 152
Conversations with Canadian Novelists 151

Corbeau 114
Corbie 114
Corvus 114
Corvus Trust 114
Covenant 154
Critical Views on Canadian Writers 143, 156
Crow 114
Cude, Wilfred 152

D

Darling, Michael 142, 143
Davidson, Arnold 143
Davies, R.R. 152
Davis, L.J. 152
Day of the Dead 25, 27
Dia de San Jose 23, 24, 26
Disher, Scott 152
Dostoyevsky 29, 144
Dube, Francine 148
Duddy Kravitz 4, 5, 12, 13, 15, 50, 51, 52, 53, 54, 55, 56, 57, 58, 61, 62, 63, 64, 74, 75, 82, 86, 93, 99, 101, 135, 141, 143, 145, 152, 153, 154, 155, 157

E

Edwards, Thomas R. 152
Eliot, T.S. 144
Ephraim 17, 110, 111, 112, 114, 118, 119, 121
Esau 6, 88
Eskimo 5, 13, 64, 65, 67, 74, 75, 114
Exodus 146, 147

F

Ferns, John 152
Fiction and Fact xi, 131, 142
Fiddlehead 153
Financial Times 153
Florence ix, 12, 13, 15, 16, 17, 49, 55, 56, 71, 75, 85, 127, 129, 130, 131, 132, 135
For Whom the Bell Tolls 2, 21, 144

Franklin Expedition 111, 147
Fraser River 89
Freedman, Adele 152
French, William 152
Frozen in Time 147
Fulford, Robert 148, 153

G

Genesis 28, 73, 144, 146
Gentile 6, 14, 34, 36, 37, 58, 79, 85
Gentiles 14, 81, 141, 157
Ghetto 100
Gilbert and Sullivan 63, 65, 76, 145
Globe and Mail 148, 149, 151, 152, 154, 156
God 3, 21, 23, 28, 29, 31, 33, 34, 35, 36, 38, 73, 83, 90, 91, 97, 106, 110, 111, 112, 116, 119
Godfrey, David 153
Gold, Joseph 153
Golem 152
Goliath 4, 53
Goodman, Walter 153
Gordon, Sheldon 153
Greenstein, Michael 143, 153

H

Haman 103
Harlow, Robert 153
Hatch, Robert 154
Heichelman, F.M. 154
Hemingway 1, 2, 21, 22, 144
Hercules 89, 90, 91, 146
Herky 88, 89
Herzog 6, 7, 122, 123, 124, 125, 127, 131, 132, 137, 147, 149
Home Sweet Home 101, 142
Honore, Carl 154
Horseman 6, 7, 14, 15, 62, 77, 87, 88, 90, 91, 92, 94, 95, 96, 97, 102, 108, 134,

135, 141, 146, 150, 151, 152, 153, 154, 156, 157
House of Israel 111
How I became an unknown 142
Hughes, Isabel 154
Hunting Tigers Under Glass 141
Hutcheon, Linda 148

I

Ibiza 10, 42, 105, 106, 107, 108
Innuit 119, 120
Irony 21, 36, 37, 66, 69, 77, 91, 94
Izzy 111

J

Jackson, Marni 154
Jacob 6, 7, 13, 15, 88, 96, 108, 149, 156
Jake 1, 87, 88, 89, 90, 91, 92, 93, 94, 95, 96, 97, 102, 134, 135, 155
Jane 135
Jason, Philip K. 154
Jeffrey, David 154
Jesus 2, 21
Jewish Chronicle 150
Jewish Quarterly 150
Jocasta 44
Johnson, William 148
Jones, Mervyn 154
Josh 100, 102, 105, 106, 108
Joshua 7, 15, 16, 17, 62, 97, 98, 99, 100, 101, 102, 104, 105, 106, 107, 108, 109, 132, 135, 141, 146, 149, 152, 153, 156, 157
Joshua Then and Now 7, 15, 17, 62, 97, 98, 99, 100, 104, 106, 108, 109, 132, 135, 141, 146, 149, 152, 153, 156
Journal of Canadian Fiction 152, 155, 156
Judaism 9, 11, 80

K

Kardonne, Rick 154

Karp 46, 47
King Lear 136, 137, 147
Knelman, Martin 154

L

Laurence, Margaret 146
Lazarus 43
Le Butt, Paul 155
Leah 3, 9, 31, 37, 38, 147, 149
Leah Rosenberg 9
Lear 136, 137, 147
Like One that Dreamed 147
Lincoln, Richard 155
London 6, 10, 12, 13, 14, 15, 16, 17, 41, 42, 45, 77, 80, 84, 85, 88, 93, 105, 111, 141, 144, 145, 147, 150, 154
Lyell, Frank 155

M

Maclean's 141, 142, 148, 149, 151, 155, 156
Mandel, E.W. 155
McClelland and Stewart 12, 13, 14, 15, 141, 142, 143, 147, 149
McKay, John 148
McSweeney, Kerry 143
Metcalf, John 155
Montreal Gazette 153
Montrealer 156
Mordecai and Me 143
Mordecai Richler Papers 145, 150, 151, 153, 154, 155, 156
Mortimer 14, 77, 78, 79, 80, 81, 82, 83, 84, 85, 145
Moses 6, 9, 16, 37, 88, 100, 101, 111, 112, 113, 115, 116, 118, 119, 120, 121
Murdoch 107
My Father's Life 101
Myers, David 155
Myers, Sean 149

N

New Statesman 151, 152
New York Times Book Review 152, 153, 155, 157
Newman, Peter C. 147
Noah 3, 11, 13, 15, 28, 29, 30, 31, 32, 33, 34, 35, 36, 37, 38, 53, 100, 133, 136, 144, 149, 153
Notes on an Endangered Species 8, 142

O

O'Reilly, Finbarr 148
Oh Canada! Oh Quebec 142
Old Testament 33, 112
Orwell, George 145
Ower, John 155
Oxford University Press 148

P

Pacey, Desmond 143
Panofsky, Ruth 155
Paris 10, 17, 126
Parody xi, xii, 1, 2, 4, 5, 6, 7, 8, 22, 23, 24, 27, 28, 33, 38, 40, 41, 43, 44, 45, 50, 51, 52, 53, 54, 57, 59, 62, 64, 66, 77, 81, 82, 86, 88, 102, 103, 105, 106, 108, 115, 119, 121, 123, 127, 135, 139, 148
Pauline 102, 105, 107, 109, 135
Perspectives on Mordecai Richler 143
Picasso 19, 144
Pollock, Zailig 143, 155
Posner, Michael 143
Promised Land 7, 55, 100, 104, 106, 108
Prose, Francine 155
Prufrock 5, 39, 40, 41, 42, 43, 45, 48, 49, 144

Q

Quebec 142, 148
Queen Esther 102
Queen's Quarterly 155

R

Rabbi Hillel 4
Raven 110, 113, 114, 115, 120, 129
Renzetti, Elizabeth 156
Richler Biographer 149
Richler, Emma 149
Richler, Jacob 149
Richler, Mordecai 141, 145
Richler, Noah 149
Rilke, Rainer Maria 144
Rooke, Leon 156
Ryerson Press 143

S

Sally 12, 40, 41, 42, 43, 45, 47, 49
Sammy 4, 5, 50, 51, 52, 53, 54, 55, 56, 57, 58, 59, 60, 61, 93, 145, 153
Satire 4, 5, 6, 13, 14, 63, 64, 68, 77, 80, 81, 82, 86, 155
Saunders, Tom 156
Schulberg, Budd 145
Seymour 68, 70, 107, 134
Shalinsky 14, 79, 80, 82, 84, 85, 145
Shoveling Trouble 87, 97, 142
Siskind, Jacob 156
Sister Crazy 149
Solomon Gursky Was Here 7, 16, 99, 110, 113, 117, 120, 121, 135, 141, 147, 150, 153, 154, 155, 156
Son of a Smaller Hero 3, 6, 11, 28, 29, 35, 38, 61, 64, 68, 69, 84, 100, 101, 133, 136, 141, 144, 150, 153, 154, 156
Sophocles 43, 48, 144
St. Urbain's Horseman 6, 7, 14, 15, 62, 77, 87, 91, 94, 96, 97, 102, 108, 134, 135, 141, 146, 150, 151, 152, 153, 154, 156, 157
Star Maker 14, 77, 78, 79, 80, 81, 83, 84, 85
Stoffman, Judy 149
Symons, A.J.A. 147

T

Talking about Books 156
Tamarack Review 68, 69, 145, 151, 152, 156
The Acrobats xi, 1, 2, 10, 19, 20, 21, 24, 25, 26, 27, 61, 64, 69, 107, 133, 136, 141, 143, 150, 153, 155
The Apprenticeship of Duddy Kravitz 4, 5, 12, 13, 15, 50, 56, 62, 63, 64, 75, 82, 86, 93, 99, 101, 135, 141, 145, 152, 153, 155, 157
The Brothers Karamazov 29, 144
The Diviners 98, 146
The Errand Runner 16, 147, 149
The Incomparable Atuk 4, 5, 6, 13, 62, 63, 64, 65, 70, 74, 76, 82, 84, 86, 118, 133, 134, 135, 141, 145, 151, 154, 157
The Nation 18, 151, 154
The Picture of Dorian Gray 41, 45, 47, 145
The Quest for Corvo 7, 113, 147
The Street 23, 24, 142
Toni 11, 21, 24, 26
Torah 30, 36, 37
Toronto Daily Star 153
Toronto Telegram 151
Trevor, William 156

U

Under the Volcano 2, 24, 25, 26, 27, 144
University of Calgary Library 68, 87, 94, 142, 145
University of Toronto Quarterly 150, 157

V

Vancouver Sun 149, 156
Vivian 45, 46, 47, 48, 49

W

Wachtel, Eleanor 156
Walker, Joan 156
Warkentin, Germaine 156
Washington Post 152
WASP 79, 80
Watmough, David 156
Watt, Frank 157
What Makes Sammy Run? 4, 5, 50, 51, 52, 54, 55, 56, 57, 58, 59, 93, 145
Wilde, Oscar 145
Williamson, David 157
Wilson, Jonathan 149
Winnipeg Free Press 156, 157
Wisse, Ruth 157
Wong, Jan 149
Woodcock, George 143
Works of Oscar Wilde 145

Y

Yanofsky, Joel 143
Yardley, John 157
Yvette 13, 54, 55, 56, 57, 58, 59, 60
Yvonne 26

Z

Ziggy 14, 79, 82

978-0-595-37208-9
0-595-37208-2

Printed in the United States
49734LVS00003B/52-78